P9-APA-182

READING PROGRESS FROM 8 TO 15

Reading Progress from 8 to 15

A survey of attainment and teaching practices in Scotland

James Maxwell

NFER Publishing Company Ltd.

095539

Published by the NFER Publishing Company Ltd.,
2 Jennings Buildings, Thames Avenue,
Windsor, Berks. SL4 1QS

Registered Office: The Mere, Upton Park, Slough, Berks. SL1 2DQ

First published 1977

© J. Maxwell, 1977

ISBN 0 85633 120 1

Printed in Great Britain by
King, Thorne and Stace Ltd., School Road, Hove, Sussex BN3 5JE

Distributed in the USA by Humanities Press Inc.,
Atlantic Highlands, New Jersey 07716 USA

Contents

095539

095539

PREFACE

This investigation was begun in 1972, financed by a grant from the Social Sciences Research Council, sponsored and assisted by the Scottish Education Department and housed in Queen Margaret College, Edinburgh. The inquiry was conducted by a Reading Research Unit of five persons, including both professional and administrative clerical staff, with a Steering Committee of persons involved in educational research, which was consulted from time to time on the progress of the inquiry. In the report which follows, any conclusions or opinions expressed are not necessarily those of the bodies mentioned above, and while the views of the Steering Committee have been taken into account throughout, the presentation in this report is that of the Reading Research Unit.

Any investigation such as this depends on the cooperation and goodwill of those involved in the work of the schools. The Unit takes this opportunity to thank all who assisted, the Directors of Education for agreeing on behalf of their Education Authorities to participate in the inquiry, those who assisted with the administration and marking of the reading tests, the Godfrey Thomson Unit for Academic Assessment, Edinburgh University, and Moray House College of Education, Dr D. A. Walker and Dr A. E. G. Pilliner for statistical advice, the Edinburgh Regional Computing Centre for assistance in tabulating data and the Office of Population, Census and Surveys, Edinburgh for their assistance in obtaining socioeconomic data from census returns. Above all, the Unit are indebted to the teachers in those schools in which the inquiry was conducted. The cooperation of the head teachers and class teachers was complete and whatever deficiencies have arisen in the conduct of the inquiry, these cannot be attributed to failure of participation by the teachers. The pupils also merit acknowledgement. They took the reading tests seriously and were full and frank in their records of their out of school reading.

Though the investigation and the report which follows is the result of the combined work of the Unit Staff, Mr Atherton has had a special involvement with the sociological aspects of the inquiry, and Mr Macleod with the recreational reading of the pupils. During the investigation the Unit Staff has been as follows:

Director:
    Mr James Maxwell, MA, MEd   (from June 1972)
Senior Research Officer:
    Mr Graham F. Atherton, BA, MA   (From May 1972)
Junior Research Officer:
    Mr Daniel S. Macleod, MA, MEd   (from May 1972
                                       to September 1975)

Administrative Officer:
    *Mrs Florence M. Cruickshanks   (from April 1972
                                       to January 1974)

    *Mr Derek T. Kilgour   (from January 1974)
    *Mr Alan R. MacGill   (from October 1975)
Clerk:
    Mrs Constance M. Reid   (from April 1972)

*on secondment from Scottish Education Department

A shorter formal report has been lodged with the Social Sciences Research Council.

Chapter 1

The Plan of the Inquiry

'My heart bleeds for anyone faced with the task of
surveying the literature of reading, which continues to
occupy its pre-eminent place in having a greater number
of researchers into its problems than is shown in any other
subject area.'   R. H. THOULESS

Not only does the learning and teaching of reading attract a large
number of researchers, but it is also the subject of many different kinds
of research ranging from surveys of children's preferences in literature
to case studies of methods used with children having reading difficulties.
The purpose of the present outline of the research procedure used is to
give the context in which the data were gathered and the conclusions
were reached. A fuller discussion of the research strategy and its implica-
tions is reserved for later chapters.

The policy of the investigation was based on four major principles,

(a)   that the selection of schools should be as extensive as possible,
so that ideally no teachers could say that the findings were irrelevant as
their kind of school was not included;

(b)   that the investigation should not be concerned with either
teaching or learning independently of each other, so that the unit
of the inquiry was neither teacher nor pupil, but the school class,
where the interaction between pupils and teachers takes place;

(c)   that the inquiry should avoid paths already well trodden.
There are libraries of reports on the early teaching of reading, and
stacks of reports on the teaching and examining of older secondary
school pupils and college or university students. The period between
has been comparatively neglected, so the investigation was planned to

cover that period of schooling between 8 and 15 years of age, or in class terms from Primary 4 to Secondary 3;

(d)   that there should be some method of objective assessment of reading attainment common to all classes, so that comparisons of progress should be on the same basis for each class.

To attain these objectives, the sample of schools was first chosen from secondary schools. Fifteen secondary schools were selected, such that they included:

(a)   Roman Catholic and non-denominational schools;
(b)   schools serving rural areas, new towns, older urban areas and residential urban areas;
(c)   schools large, medium and small in number of pupils on the roll;
(d)   schools with and without their own primary department;
(e)   single sex and mixed schools;
(f)   local authority and grant aided schools.

The selection was made before the transfer of schools to regional authorities and the phasing out of assistance to grant aided schools. There is some overlap of the categories of schools, for example the only single sex schools were also grant aided. Independent schools, special schools and schools in the Highlands and Islands were not included. From these schools, 58 'feeder'' primary schools were identified, ranging from one-teacher rural schools to larger city schools, some in old premises, others in very new.

All the primary 4 classes in these schools, 99 classes in all, make up the first sample of classes. These were followed through from the beginning of their P4 year in 1972 to the end of their P6 year in 1975. Of these 99 classes, 82 survived into the P7 stage as substantially the same class, the remainder being lost through closing of schools, re-organization of classes and the fact that some rural schools transferred pupils after the P5 stage. This group of classes, containing about 2,500 pupils constitutes the younger group in the investigation. The other and older group, also containing about 2,500 pupils, was made up of the 97 primary 7 classes in the same primary schools. These pupils were followed through from the beginning of the P7 stage in 1972 to the end of their second year in the secondary school. In the secondary schools the one to one relationship between teacher and class does not prevail, so the pupil teacher relationship was examined by selecting representative teachers from the main subject areas in the secondary school.

By joining the two groups, P4 to P6 and P7 to S2, a survey of the reading teaching of the upper primary and lower secondary classes can be made for certain aspects at least. In some parts of the report which follows, primary and secondary practices have had to be considered separately but where possible, as in the discussion of out of school reading, they have been combined.

The testing of the reading attainments of the classes was done by using the Edinburgh Reading Tests. This is a series with different tests according to the ages of the pupils. Stage 2 is for pupils aged 8:6 to 10:6, Stage 3 for ages 10:0 to 12:6 and Stage 4 for ages 12:0 to 16:0 years of age. Each stage consists of several subtests (not the same for each stage) such as Vocabulary, Comprehension of Essential Ideas, Use of Context and so on. These subtests, however, do not appear to distinguish clearly between the different components in reading skills; the total score on each stage of the tests was taken as a broad indication of reading attainment. The attainments covered by the Edinburgh Reading Tests extend somewhat beyond a strict definition of reading as such and include some elements of general language.

The reading tests were administered in September or October of each year session, according to the following schedule:

Session	Class	ERT Stage
1972/3	P4	2
1973/4	P5	2
1975/6	P7	3
1972/3	P7	3
1975/6	S3	3 or 4

The results of the tests given to the P4 and to the P7 classes at the outset of the investigation were discussed with the class teachers, who were asked to say whether the test score agreed with their personal assessment of the pupils' attainments. The differences of opinion are given overleaf, where 'plus' means the teacher considered a pupils' reading to be better than the test score indicated, and 'minus' that the pupil was worse.

Most of the differences in assessment were comparatively small, arising for the most part from the situation where two pupils that the teacher considered to be of equal attainment had differences in test score. In these the teachers tended to upgrade the pupil with the poorer

Table 1.1: Class teacher's agreement with reading test score

		Per cent Plus	*Per cent Minus*
P4	Boys	16	5
	Girls	17	4
P7	Boys	9	4
	Girls	11	2

score. Hence the larger number of plus entries. The greater discrepancies between teacher and test recorded for P4 are probably due to the fact that P4 teachers' estimates were partly based on oral reading, which was not an element of the test. Perfect agreement between test score and teachers' estimates is not to be expected. But disagreement is neither frequent nor substantial, so that by and large the test scores can be used as a measure of reading attainment which is acceptable to the class teachers.

Various bits of information can be extracted from the records of pupils' reading test scores. The raw score is the total mark obtained on a test. Where two different reading tests are used, as in P4 and P7 who used Stage 2 and Stage 3 respectively, a direct comparison of scores is not possible, but a relative comparison is permissible in that if two classes have the same average raw score in the P4 test but one has a higher score than the other in the P7 test three years later, the first class can be said to have made more progress in reading attainment than the other. The difficulty is that it is not possible to say precisely how much more progress. Another measure that can be obtained from the test scores is the reading quotient. This quotient indicates how a pupil has performed on the reading test in comparison with pupils of the same age. A group of pupils each may have a reading quotient of 100, but the older pupils will have a higher level of reading attainment in terms of Raw Score, because they are older and the quotient includes an allowance for age differences. Comparison between reading quotients is possible between different tests, but once again it is not possible to measure the actual amount of improvement. What is possible, is to say that a pupil whose RQ (reading quotient) was 100 in P4 and 100 in P7 has probably improved in reading competence between P4 and P7, but that other pupils have improved by the same amount, so that the pupil still remains average for his age.

In general the raw score has been given preference over reading quotient in the investigation, because raw score is a more direct assessment of the pupils' competence. In the primary school classes, only 2·6 per cent of the pupils fell outwith a range of 12 months of age, and teachers did not appear to make special allowance for age differences within the span of one year. Where more appropriate, however, quotients have been used. From these two measures certain characteristics of the pupils and classes can be identified. The data may be presented in terms of all pupils in the sample, referred to as the population, or of classes in the sample, where the data are presented in terms of class averages. An apparent discrepancy may be mentioned here. For the P7 sample in 1972 the average RQ of the 2518 pupils was 98·05 whereas the mean RQ of the 99 class averages was 97·7. The small difference in the two averages is due to different methods of calculation. Another set of data obtained from test scores concerns the range of differences between pupils or classes. The amount of difference is measured by Standard Deviation (SD). A class with a large standard deviation of raw score, for example, contains pupils with a wider range of reading attainment than a class with a small standard deviation. Reading quotients are standardized for a population to give the mean as 100 and the standard deviation as 15.

Finally, the production of the Edinburgh Reading Tests and the conduct of the investigation were proceeding concurrently, with the result that the Reading Tests had to be used on some occasions before their properties were fully known. This added some complications to the investigation, for example where it was found that in P4 classes, the test failed to distinguish between poor and very poor readers. This was corrected by a second administration of the test in P5, which in fact added information to the inquiry, but makes the presentation of the findings that little bit more complex.

Though some time has been devoted to discussion of the testing programme, by which reading attainment and progress has been assessed, the test scores are only one item of the inquiry into the teaching of reading. Other aspects of the topic investigated include school and class organization, teachers' views and practices concerning the teaching of reading, the class books used, not only for teaching reading the provisions for remedial teaching, the socio-economic differences between good and poor readers, the reading demands of secondary school subject teachers, the experience, qualifications and training of primary school teachers and the leisure reading of the pupils. These components of the investigation are too extensive to discuss at this point, and how they were identified will emerge as the report proceeds.

Chapter 2

The Teaching of Reading in Primary School Classes

'As one turns to the information about schools and schooling, the results are somewhat disheartening as far as providing cues as to what aspects of a school organization or program contribute to the reading ability of the children in the school. In general, the factors that it was possible to identify in the school are at best minimally related to reading achievement.'   R. L. THORNDIKE

How good at reading are Scottish pupils?

One of the first questions that is asked about any study of reading is, how good is the teaching of reading in Scotland? This question cannot readily be answered in Scotland alone; comparison with other countries can give at least an approximate answer. The quotation above sums up one part of the findings of an international inquiry* into 'Reading Comprehension Education in Fifteen Countries', of which Scotland was one. A population of ten-year-olds and a population of fourteen-year-olds were given reading comprehension tests, in the appropriate language and roughly equivalent in difficulty. The results for the ten-year-olds showed Scotland fourth equal with England after Sweden, Italy and Finland, and for the fourteen-year-olds, third equal with Belgium (French), Finland and USA, after New Zealand and Italy. International comparisons are full of pitfalls, language differences and sampling differences (as in Italy where the more retarded readers were omitted), but they are the best estimates available. Whether Scotland's position in the league table is good enough is a matter of opinion; at least Scotland does appear as one of the more illiterate nations. Both Stage 2 and Stage 3 of the Edinburgh Reading Tests were stan-

*International Studies in Evaluation III, R. L. Thorndike, IEA (1973).

dardized separately for Scotland and for England and Wales and whatever the differences between Scottish and English and Welsh education
the differences in average reading attainment are very small.

Another finding of the international comparison study is that educational provision in Scotland for ten-year-olds is very uniform, exceeded
only by Sweden and equalled by England. This finding is confirmed by
the present Scottish investigation in which it has been found that
differences in reading attainment are very much greater within classes
than between classes. This finding means that there are very few, if any,
primary schools or classes in Scotland which are outstandingly better or
worse than the others. For fourteen-year-olds, the international comparison shows a greater diversity among secondary schools. This inquiry
was launched in 1966, and during the last ten years the changes in
organization and practices in Scottish secondary schools have been
much greater than those in primary schools so that the findings of the
international comparison in this area are of doubtful validity.

Is the standard of reading improving ?

In England and Wales the National Foundation for Educational
Research (NFER) have conducted periodical surveys of reading standards
of eleven-year-old pupils. The report of the latest (1970) survey*
showed that the steady increase in reading test scores from 1948 had now
ceased, and there was, if anything, a slight deterioration in reading
standards. This finding caused some controversy and contributed to the
setting up of the Bullock Committee to inquire into the teaching of reading in England and Wales. These periodical surveys of reading standards were not conducted in Scotland, so the sources of information
about changes in reading standards are very limited. In the present investigation, however, a comparison between reading standards, as
measured by Edinburgh Reading Test Stage 3, is possible between P7
pupils at the beginning of session 1972/3 and session 1975/6. The
difference over this rather short period is given below in terms of
Reading Quotients. Grant aided schools are not included.

		Number	Mean RQ
1972/3	Boys	1167	96·6
	Girls	1161	96·5
	Both	2328	96·6
1975/6	Boys	1121	97·5
	Girls	1115	96·7
	Both	2236	97·1

*The Trend of Reading Standards, K. B. Start and B. K. Wells, NFER, 1972.

The average performance in 1975 was 0·5 points of RQ better than in 1972. This is negligibly small. The conclusion to be reached is that there has been no significant change in P7 reading standards between 1972 and 1975.

Different aspects of primary school reading

To enable some orderly examination of the different parts reading plays in the primary school pupils activity, the reading is considered here as following three main streams. These can be called, for identification in the discussion, literary reading, functional reading and recreational reading. Functional reading is that which is used for studies other than that explicity taught as reading. The reading of instructions, or the reading involved in mathematics and project work is included in functional reading. Recreational reading is defined as the reading done by pupils for their own purposes and interest, and done without school requirements. Such reading included comics and newspapers as well as books, and is selected by the pupil. Functional and recreational reading are discussed later in this report, so that the present discussion refers to the reading which is explicitly taught by the class teachers. In all classes this was based mainly on the use of class readers, and the word 'literary' has been used because by far the largest components in these readers are passages of continuous prose with occasional poems or dramatic extracts.

Though most teachers used class readers, there were differences of opinion among teachers about their use. The majority regarded reading as an integral part of the wider area of language teaching, a minority regarded reading as a separate skill to be taught as such. Others adopted on intermediate mixed practice. The trend in primary education has been towards teaching language arts rather than to maintain the separate teaching of reading, writing, spelling and so on. The incidence of the different practices is given in Table 2.1 as percentages.

Table 2.1: Teaching of reading and writing

	P4	P5	P6	:	P7
Integrated	63	77	86	:	69
Mixed	21	16	12	:	20
Separated	15	7	2	:	11
No. Teachers	(71)	(96)	(101)	:	(75)

The trend from P4 through P5 to P6 (which are the same classes at different stages) is evident. As the pupils grow older less emphasis is being placed on the teaching of reading as a separate skill and more on integration in general language teaching. Perhaps also there is a secular trend in the schools towards less specific teaching of reading. The P7 records were taken in the same year as the P4, namely 1972, the P5 and P6 records applying to 1973 and 1974 respectively. Also there are about twice as many longer service teachers taking P7 classes as teach P4.

The teachers' emphasis is on integration of language teaching, but the critical question is whether it produces better results. In this investigation, attainment and progress are assessed in terms of a test, broadly based though it is, which is essentially a test of reading competence. The question can only be answered for reading not for general language competence. It is appropriate here to introduce a form of presentation used at intervals throughout this report. Classes can be put in a rank order in terms of the average raw score or reading quotient, or the differences between average score on one occasion and another. The system adopted is to label the top quarter of the classes as A classes, the bottom quarter as C classes and the middle half as B classes. The use of class averages implies grouping by the general level of class attainment or progress; all pupils in A classes are not necessarily above average in reading. Very small classes are omitted.

It is the convention in research work to test the statistical significance of findings. The term 'significance' is here a technical one and does not refer to the importance of the findings. A difference for example is significant if it is unlikely to have happened by chance. If the chances are less than one in twenty that a relationship or difference could be a chance one, it is said to be significant at $p = \cdot 05$ level. If the probability of a chance relationship or difference is less than one in one hundred $p = \cdot 01$. In the next table (2.2) 'Integration of Reading and Writing by Reading Progress and Attainment' it appears as if the separate/mixed classes tend to show better progress than the integrated classes, in that $5/12$ of the separate/mixed classes are in the A quarter as against $7/40$ of the integrated classes. It is quite possible that the separated/mixed practice is associated with more progress in reading, but the relationship is not strong enough to exclude chance. A test of statistical significance on the figures in the table shows that chance is a possible explanation that cannot be ruled out, as p is greater than $\cdot 05$. The relationship is therefore described as non-significant, that is, it may be real or it may be chance. As many of the relationships examined in the report are not significant statistically, only when the relationships are statistically significant will that be stated.

To return to the original question of whether integration of reading and writing teaching produces better results on the reading test, the tables below give the data for those classes who have had integrated teaching throughout the three years from P4 to P6, and those who have had separate or mixed practice for two of the three years. Only one class did not have some integrated teaching. The upper part of the table gives the comparison for progress between P4 and P7, the A classes having the largest differences between average Raw Scores in P4 and P7 and the c classes the smallest. The lower part gives the A B C classification for the end result, the raw score on the reading test in P7.

Table 2.2: Integration of reading and writing by reading progress and attainment

	A	B	C	Total
Progress P4 – P7				
All integrated	7	25	8	40
⅔ separate or mixed	5	4	3	12
Attainment P7	A	B	C	Total
All integrated	9	21	10	40
⅔ separate or mixed	5	4	3	12

The main differences appear in the A classes, those who have made most progress or have reached the highest attainment level in P7. This suggests that the teaching of reading as a specific skill may be a more effective way of producing good readers than is integration of language studies. This is one of the findings of the investigation which cannot be regarded as conclusive; a further controlled experiment would be needed to establish firm conclusions.

Are class size and composition related to reading progress and attainment?

Class size is defined as the number of pupils in charge of the teacher, whose duty was the teaching of reading. If those pupils were all at the same stage in their schooling, P5 for example, the class is called homogeneous. If the class contains pupils at different stages, P5 and P6 for example, the class is called composite, but the total number of P5 and P6 pupils is recorded as class size, or more precisely, pupils per teacher.

During the period of the investigation the average number of pupils per teacher was of the order of 30 to 31, but towards the end of this period pressure for smaller classes was mounting, which appears as a decrease in the number of large classes. As the Table 2.3 indicates, this had only a small effect on the average number of pupils per teacher (ppt). The smaller classes are mostly in rural schools.

Table 2.3: Number of pupils per teacher

Class	Average ppt	Range of ppt	Session
P4	30·1	15–45	1972/3
P5	31·2	12–44	1973/4
P6	29·9	18–39	1974/5
P7	30·2	16–43	1972/3

Whether these differences in class size shown above as the range of pupils per teacher are related to reading attainment and progress is shown in Table 2.4. A correlation coefficient of $r=0$ means no relationship.

Table 2.4: Reading progress and attainment by class size

Difference P4 and P5 test scores and ppt in P4	$r = +0·01$
Difference P5 and P7 RQ and ppt in P5	$r = -0·02$
Difference P5 and P7 RQ and ppt in P6	$r = -0·02$
P7 Mean RQ per class and ppt in P6	$r = -0·06$

None of the correlation coefficients is significantly different from zero, the conclusion being that within a range of about 15 to 45 pupils per teacher, class size is unrelated to pupils' progress and attainment in reading in the upper primary school. Nearly all previous inquiries have reached the same conclusion, so this finding is not unexpected.

The movement towards smaller classes was effected mainly by reducing the size of larger homogeneous classes and creating a larger number of composite classes of smaller size. The trend is shown in Table 2.5. Composite classes are the normal thing in smaller and rural schools, but the number of such schools decreased as the inquiry proceeded.

Table 2.5: Number of composite classes per session

Class	No. Composite Classes	No. all Classes	Session
P4	21	99	1972/3
P5	36	101	1973/4
P6	41	110	1974/5
P7	14	97	1972/3

The increase in composite classes appears most markedly in P5, so it is possible to assess how far the introduction of more composite classes between P5 and P7 effects the progress of pupils between P5 and P7 and their final attainment level in P7. Minus differences are those less than average P5 to P7 difference.

Table 2.6: Composite and homogeneous classes P5, P6, P7 RQs

Class	Mean RQ P7	Difference RQ P5/P7	Mean No. ppt P5	P6
Composite P4–P5–P6 ($n=10$)	97·6	−0·7	26·2	25·8
Homogeneous P4–P5–P6 ($n=44$)	99·3	+0·5	32·0	31·4
Homogeneous in P4 to Composite in P5 and/or P6 ($n=17$)	95·4	−0·5	33·3	30·9

Changing from homogeneous to composite classes to reduce class size appears to give no advantage to the pupils in either reading progress or attainment. The classes changed in P5 or P6 from homogeneous to composite show a reduction in average size, 33·3 to 30·9 pupils per teacher, but this is accompanied by progress of one point reading quotient less and a final reading quotient 3·9 less than the continuing homogeneous classes. The results of this investigation give no support to the view that reduction in class sizes by creating smaller composite classes benefits the pupils as far as reading is concerned.

Pupil and teacher turnover

Frequent change of teacher is generally considered to have an adverse effect on pupils' education. In the classes in this investigation the amount of teacher turnover was so small that no conclusions could be reached. Taking the definition of teacher turnover as more than two teachers per session, in P4, three per cent of the classes were so affected, in P5 no classes were reported as affected, in P6 three per cent and in P7 two per cent of the classes reported turnover. The change of teacher does not appear as a major factor in pupils' school experience. No class reported teacher turnover for more than one of the three sessions.

Substantial changes in the personnel of a class may break continuity of teaching and may have an adverse effect on the progress of the class as a whole. Though pupil turnover is a continuous process, it was not thought necessary nor profitable to keep week-by-week records of class rolls. Pupil turnover has therefore been calculated on the changes occurring between one testing session and the next, in such a way that a class of forty pupils which lost ten pupils and gained eight would be recorded as having a turnover of 30 per cent (average of 10 plus 8, divided by 30 remaining pupils.

Whether the pupil turnover is related to class attainment in reading is shown in Table 2.7, the ABC classification being for P5 and P7 respectively.

Table 2.7: Pupil turnover and reading attainment

	A	B	C	All	Class Tested
% turnover (P4–P5)	14	21	23	19	P5
% turnover (P5–P7)	23	29	19	25	P7

The P5 results show a slight tendency towards lesser turnover in the better classes, but the P7 results show a similar slight tendency in the opposite direction. The only conclusion possible is that pupil turnover and reading attainment level are not related to each other.

A similar comparison between turnover and pupils' progress between P4 and P5 and between P5 and P7 confirms this conclusion. Again there is no relationship between the two variables, both correlation coefficients not differing significantly from zero.

Analysis of the test scores of pupils leaving and pupils entering the classes, shows that the two groups of pupils are of much the same level of attainment, so that the classes, though containing different pupils remain of the same level and range of ability. As school catchment areas were not substantially changed either, it is reasonable to assume that the incoming and outgoing pupils have much the same kind of home background. Compared with the influences of ability and home background, the effects of pupil turnover on reading attainment and progress are very marginal.

Class organization and reading progress

Teachers had a choice of three main systems of class organization for the teaching of reading. These were reported as class teaching, group teaching or individual teaching. Mixed organization was of course, possible, and in the smaller rural schools the teacher's choice of organization was limited by the school organization.

As the pupils progressed from P4 to P7 some changes in incidence of different organization was evident.

Table 2.8: Class organization P4 – P7

Organization	P4(1972/3)	P5(1973/4)	P6(1974/5)	P7(1972/3
Class only	2	8	6	9
Group only	10	44	16	17
Individual only	8	11	4	3
Class + Group	3	4	10	8
Class + Individual	10	11	13	19
Group + Individual	49	23	38	28
Class + Group + Individual	16	2	17	12
Total	98	103	104	96

The P5 classes, for some reason not discovered, seem to be the odd man out. Apart from that there are only very general trends to be observed in the table above. Group teaching, either alone or in combination, is the most popular approach, though it is to some extent superseded by class teaching in the latter years of the primary school.

As the classes progress through P4, P5 and P6 class organization appears to change according to the teachers' preferences. Only two classes, both group only, were consistently taught under the same organization for three years. The others all experienced changes in class organization as they moved through the school. Of these, eight classes received class teaching, but not exclusively so for all three years, similarly 47 received some group and 13 some individual teaching for the same period. If the ABC classification for P7 reading test score and for progress from P4 to P7 is applied to these classes, Table 2.9 results.

On balance, individual teaching appears to lead to more favourable results, but too much importance should not be attached to this, as the individual teaching was nearly always accompanied by some group or class teaching or both.

Ability grouping

Of more interest are certain features within these class organizations. Where group teaching is practised, the groups can be constituted on

Table 2.9: Class organization and reading attainment and progress

(a) Some class teaching for all three years

	A	B	C	Total
P7 Test Score	1	3	4	8
P4–P7 Progress	1	4	3	8

(b) Some group teaching for all three years

	A	B	C	Total
P7 Test Score	10	22	15	47
P4–P7 Progress	10	24	13	47

(c) Some individual teaching for all three years

	A	B	C	Total
P7 Test Score	4	6	3	13
P4–P7 Progress	4	6	3	13

various principles. The most common is grouping by pupils' ability. The international inquiry into Reading Comprehension Education in Fifteen Countries, already referred to, found a fairly consistent negative relationship between the practice of ability grouping and reading comprehension. In the present investigation, where group organization was practiced, the classes were divided into those using only ability grouping, and the others. There were no significant differences in attainment or progress between the two sets of classes. The conclusion is that grouping by ability is not necessarily associated with better reading performance.

Individual teaching of good and poor readers

Another matter of interest is the basis on which pupils are selected for individual teaching of reading. Poor readers only were selected by 146 teachers from P4 to P7, and four teachers selected good readers only, three of them being in P6. Seven teachers selected only both good and poor readers for individual attention. The discrepancy between the individual attention given to poor as against good readers is therefore of the order of fourteen to one. The number of pupils of a high level of reading ability who receive individual attention from their teachers is very small indeed. Whether this is a matter of educational policy, or whether teachers are unaware of the discrepancy is not clear. If it is intentional then the more able pupils have grounds for complaint. If it is not intentional policy, then there

are valid criticisms of teachers for not devoting an appropriate proportion of their attention to their most able readers, and for being
apparently unaware of the guidance that is needed and can be given
to develop and extend the reading abilities of their best readers. In
view of the remedial services in many schools also available for poor
readers, there seems little justification for this imbalance between the
poorer and the better readers.

Open plan and team teaching

Two schools operated a system of team teaching of English broadly
akin to ability grouping within a class, but in these cases spread over
two or three combined classes. Four schools were open plan at the end
of the inquiry but only one at the outset. As none of the pupils were
throughout the P4 to P7 period subjected to established practice of
team teaching or open plan schooling, any assessment of the effects of
these practices would be premature. In the open plan schools the
teachers' initial response was on balance favourable. The common view
as expressed by teachers in interview was that the increased flexibility of
organization was welcome, but the increased noise was not.

Teachers' views on the teaching of reading

Teachers' aims in teaching reading

The class teachers were each asked to state what were the main
features they aimed at developing in the teaching of reading. The
question was open ended and the views recorded in the teachers' own
words. There was a great deal of agreement among teachers in the
terms they used to express their aims, and classification of the most
frequent responses was easy. Table 2.10 gives the most frequent

Table 2.10: Teachers' aims in teaching reading (number and responses)

Aim	P4(1972/3)	P5(1973/4)	P6(1974/5)	P7(1972/3)	All
Interest/Enjoyment	38	52	66	47	203
Comprehension	24	22	30	20	96
Skills	37	16	22	22	97
Vocational/Practical	10	28	5	9	52
Fluency	7	6	7	7	27
Information	19	16	12	18	65
Others	21	11	1	18	51
All	156	151	143	141	591

responses, and as many teachers gave more than one response, the number of responses is greater than the number of teachers. The classifications are not discrete, but are as given by teachers. Usually, 'skills' referred to 'basic' and 'phonic' skills rather than to the more advanced skills, and tended to refer to poorer readers.

A clearer picture can perhaps be obtained by broader classification into three main groups. Interest and enjoyment constitute one group, comprehension another and the third group, the skills group combines skills, practical/vocational and fluency. Learning to read for information falls between comprehension and skills, and is therefore omitted from the main groups. Expressing the frequency as percentages, the incidence of the three groups of aims is as below.

Table 2.11:

	P4	P5	P6	P7
Interest/enjoyment	33	42	51	45
Comprehension	21	18	23	19
Skills	46	40	26	36
Total %	100	100	100	100

Keeping in mind that P7 refers to an earlier session (1972/3) than P5 or P6, there is a broad trend towards greater emphasis on Interest and Enjoyment and lesser emphasis on Skills as the pupils progress through the school. This confirms the impression gained during the visits to the schools, namely that the teachers' meaning of skills referred mainly to the basic or phonic skills needed for the mechanics of reading, but was not seriously concerned with the teaching of the next level of reading skills. What these skills are is still a matter of debate, but there was little sign in the schools that the teachers in the upper primary classes had given the matter much consideration. The effect of this lack of development of new skills after the pupil can read the descriptive-narrative type of material found in class readers has already been mentioned in connection with the relative absence of individual attention for good readers, and will be referred to later in the context of the reading requirements in the secondary school.

Teachers' aims by class organization

The question is whether these teachers who emphasize the Interest/ Enjoyment component in reading tend to favour one kind of class organization rather than another. The basic distinction in class organization is between class teaching and group teaching, and the teachers have been divided into two categories, those who include some class teaching and those who include some group teaching. Teachers who practised both appear twice. The results of the analysis are expressed as ratios of class to group organization, such that more group than class teaching would give a value of less than one, and conversely.

Table 2.12: Teachers' aims by class organization

Aims	P4	P5	P6	P7
Interest/Enjoyment	0·4	0·2	0·6	0·7
Comprehension	0·5	0·6	0·5	1·4
Skills	0·3	0·7	0·6	0·9
All responses	0·4	0·3	0·6	0·7

Apart from a tendency for more class teaching in the P6 and P7 classes, there is no evidence that different teaching aims express themselves in different class organization.

Teachers' aims by integration of reading and writing

The question here is whether differences in teachers' aims are expressed in their practice of integrating reading into the general teaching of language, or teaching reading in part as a separate skill. This distinction has been discussed above, and the classification of aims mentioned remains the same. To obtain a general view, the returns for all four classes, P4, P5, P6 and P7, have been combined. The result is as in Table 2.13.

Table 2.13: Reading/writing practice

Aims	Integrated	Separate/Mixed
Interest/Enjoyment	136	43
Comprehension	60	31
Skills	89	25
	285	99

There is no significant relationship between the teachers' aims and practices here.

Only four classes were taught from P4 to P7 by different teachers holding the same views. The typical pupil encountered teachers aiming at developing different aspects of reading. This variety of emphasis makes it impossible to relate teachers' aims to pupils' progress from P4 to P7, but at no point where assessment of reading attainment was made was there any clear relationship between teachers' aims and the average reading attainment of their classes.

Teachers' views on differences between good and poor readers

The class teachers were asked for their opinions why, of a group of pupils entering school and receiving the same education, some became good readers and others poor. The responses were recorded as given by the teachers, and again it was easy to classify the majority of them, and again several teachers gave more than one response. A table of the responses is in Table 2.14.

Table 2.14: Teachers' reasons for good and poor reading

Reason	P4 (1972/3)	P5 (1973/4)	P6 (1974/5)		P7 (1972/3)
Home Background	65	53	49	:	66
Natural Ability	34	37	32	:	39
Early Training	18	24	12	:	20
Interest	12	19	11	:	8
Personality	9	9	0	:	6
Maturity	3	3	0	:	0
Others	7	4	14	:	9
All	148	149	118	:	148

There is little evidence of any change of opinion by teachers according to the stage of the class they teach. Home background and natural ability together account for more than fifty per cent of the reasons given. There is no apparent relationship between the teachers' views as expressed above and their systems of class organization. Also, the pupils, as they progress from P4 to P7 are taught by teachers expressing such a variety of views on good and poor readers, that only two classes were taught throughout by teachers who held the same views. It is therefore, unprofitable to try to relate teachers views to their classes' progress or attainment in reading.

Teachers, who have an involvement in education, might be expected to lay greatest stress on the effects of teaching, but do not in fact do so. Though the teachers were probably unaware of it, their opinions reflect frequent research findings, such as that quoted at the head of this chapter, that educational progress is determined much more by the nature of the intake, in terms of ability and home background, than by differences in educational treatment.

Consistency of teachers' estimates

As the most favoured reason for the difference between good and poor readers was home background, it is interesting to try to check how far the teachers' estimates of the effects of home background on their pupils are consistent and valid. The teachers were asked to assess whether the encouragement to read given by the home was satisfactory for all or most of their pupils, for about half of their pupils, or for few or none. The assessments were for substantially the same set of pupils progressing from P4 through P5 and P6. Unless there were very marked changes in home attitudes for most of the pupils in a class over these three years, which is very unlikely, the expectation is that the teachers' estimates would be the same for the pupils whether they were in class P4, P5 or P6. The results are shown in Table 2.15, where the ABC classification for class attainment and progress has been used.

Table 2.15: Teachers' estimates of satisfactory home encouragement by class reading attainment and progress

Pupils receiving home encouragement	*A*	*B*	*C*	*All*	*Class Tested*	
All or most	10	3	0	13	P7	
	8	4	1	13	P4–7	Progress
About half	0	2	0	2	P7	
	0	2	0	2	P4–7	Progress
Few or none	0	6	4	10	P7	
	1	4	5	10	P4–7	Progress
No consistency	2	6	3	11	P7	
	2	6	3	11	P4–7	Progress

Of the 81 classes which continued from P4 to P7, 25 had teachers whose estimates were consistent over the three years. These are recorded above. There were 11 classes whose teachers recorded three different estimates for the three years. These are 'no consistency'. The remainder gave mixed estimates. This is not an impressive record of consistent estimation by different teachers for the same kind of pupils coming from the same kind of homes. On the other hand, there is a clear and significant tendency for teachers to relate good attainment and progress to satisfactory home encouragement. This corroborates, but does not prove the teachers' emphasis on home background as an important influence on reading attainment and progress. But the data above suggest strongly that teachers are not very reliable at judging the home situation when it applies in their own classes. Only 30 per cent of the classes are given the same teachers' estimate over the three years.

Teachers' estimates of language level of class

Teachers' standards of judgment of the degree of satisfactoriness of home encouragement vary widely. Another similar assessment made by the teachers concerned the level of language competence in their classes. Differences in language level can be attributed either to natural ability or home background, but there is still a marked inconsistency in teachers' judgment. Of the 81 classes, 29 were judged either as Satisfactory, or as less than Satisfactory consistently over the three years. Also, for the twenty-two classes judged as satisfactory, there was no clear relationship between teachers' judgment and class progress or attainment in reading. The seven classes judged consistently to be of less than satisfactory level of language competence, however, were significantly poorer than others in both reading attainment in P7 and progress between P4 and P7.

Once again, there is very wide variation among teachers' opinion of the language competence of the same class. It may be that classes do change, but if the two reading tests given in P4 and P7 are taken as measuring language competence, part of which they do, then of the 19 classes showing most improvement only five show a parallel improvement in the teachers' estimates of language level, and of the 19 classes showing least improvement, only three show a parallel lack of improvement in the teachers' estimates; in fact five show teachers' estimates going in the opposite direction.

Reliability and validity of teachers' estimates

This unreliability of teachers' estimates of home encouragement and language level of their classes is more than a research curiosity. It is probable that class teachers are able to make valid assessments of the language levels of different children within their classes. There is sub-

095539

stantial agreement between teachers' estimates and Reading Test scores (Table 1.1). It is unreasonable to expect teachers to estimate the standing of their classes in comparison with classes in other schools, and as the data above indicate, judgments fluctuate widely. This may have misleading effects when information is passed from one teacher to the next, and most of all when pupils transfer from primary to secondary school.

'We are in no doubt of the importance of monitoring standards of achievement in literacy, and of doing so by the most sophisticated methods possible' (Bullock Report 3.2). The context of the Bullock Committee's recommendation is the periodical monitoring of national standards, but the same principle applies equally to the assessment of standards at any given time. No properly constructed test, whatever its limitations, would produce the fluctuating and conflicting opinions derived from teachers' estimates. An investigation such as this was possible because some common standard of reading attainment for all schools, in this case the Edinburgh Reading Tests, was available. If assessment of pupils' progress and attainment had depended on teacher's estimates, no conclusions could have been reached.

This is not a criticism of teachers' judgment; teachers cannot be expected to compare their class with other unknown classes. There is a case for a uniform assessment of pupils' literacy over all schools and classes; the findings of this inquiry not only support the Bullock recommendation, but would also extend it.

The other aspect discussed here, the teachers' estimates of home encouragement is more difficult. It is very seldom that teachers' estimates are based on direct observation of the home. Mostly it is by inference from the pupils' performance in the classroom, supplemented by occasional meeting with parents. Here the teachers' judgments of the home attitudes are more suspect. It is not unknown from other research inquiries for two teachers to reach different assessment of home encouragement and attitudes based on two different members of the same family. In this respect, therefore, even teachers' estimates of home conditions of their own pupils may be unreliable. The question of whether it is possible to obtain an assessment of home conditions similar to a test of language or reading competence is a very difficult one, and is discussed more fully later in the report. Suffice it to say here that the teachers' estimates of home encouragement need to be interpreted with great caution. They may be correct in the importance they attach to the home attitudes and conditions, but it is very doubtful if they can define and measure that influence on their pupils' reading achievement.

095533

Teachers' assessment of reading

Still on the subject of assessment, the ways by which the teachers assessed the reading progress of their pupils were remarkably uniform. Of the 376 teachers recording information for P4 to P7 classes, 360 used continuous assessment of class work as their method of assessment. Of these 360, there were 71 who supplemented continuous assessment with weekly or less frequent tests. Regular testing only was recorded by 16 teachers, eight of them for P7 classes. No teachers recorded regular use of standardized reading tests, but a large number of teachers welcomed the application of standardized reading tests used in this investigation, and none refused to participate. It appeared that the difficulty about using standardized tests was not one of principle, but of expense.

Practices in teaching reading

It is not the custom for Scottish teachers to adopt 'ready-made' schemes or systems of teaching reading, as happens in USA for example. There are a few such systems available in UK, but these are all for the earlier stages of reading. The only structured material for the upper primary classes are of the 'Reading Laboratory' type, the only ones mentioned being the SRA and the Ward Lock series. The use of these is discussed under the heading of class books rather than teaching practices. The main practices investigated were the integrating of reading with written language, already discussed, the use of oral reading, formal silent reading and reading homework.

Oral reading

There were two aspects of oral reading investigated, reading by pupils to teacher, mainly for teaching and assessment, and reading by teacher to pupils, mainly consisting of stories, with some poetry.

The practice of hearing the pupils read remains at much the same level of incidence over P4, P5 and P6, but shows a falling off in P7.

Table 2.16: Oral reading: pupil to teacher (percentages)

Oral Reading	P4	P5	P6	:	P7
Regular	86	91	82	:	48
Occasional	11	8	17	:	40
None	4	1	1	:	12

The high frequency of oral reading by pupils enables the classes where regular oral reading was practised over the three years P4 – P6 to be identified. Of 82 classes, 56 continued regular oral reading throughout. There was, however, no relationship between regular oral reading by pupils and class attainment and progress in reading over these three years.

The pattern of the other practice, oral reading by teacher to pupils is very similar, considerably less being done in P7. The percentages for regular reading by the teacher for P4, P5, P6 and P7 are respectively, 78 per cent, 75 per cent, 74 per cent and 36 per cent. Again the 29 classes where it was the regular practice over three years showed no significant differences in attainment and progress from the others.

Differences between P4, P5 and P6 are insignificant, nearly all pupils either reading aloud or listening to the teacher reading in most of their classes. In P7 there is a marked drop in the amount of both types of oral reading. As no class went through the P4 – P6 stages with consistently no oral reading of either type, it is not possible to assess the value of the practice in terms of relative progress in reading achievement.

Formal silent reading

The word formal is used to denote the practice where a specified period was set aside for the purpose of silent reading. In all classes some silent reading was encouraged by the teachers, for example use of class libraries after assigned tasks had been completed, but not all teachers prescribed set periods for class silent reading. The incidence of formal silent reading is given in Table 2.17.

Table 2.17: Formal silent reading (percentages)

Silent Reading	P4	P5	P6	:	P7
Regular	84	73	80	:	66
Occasional	8	17	13	:	18
None	8	10	7	:	16

Once again, P7 classes show some reduction in frequency of regular silent reading. In view of the definition used here it should not be assumed that P7 classes do less silent reading; it may only mean less direct prescription of silent reading as a class exercise. As with oral reading, pupils receiving regular silent reading for all three years show no significant difference in reading attainment or progress from the others.

Reading homework

The information asked for was whether the class was given regular, occasional or no homework which involved some reading. Those teachers giving regular home work were further asked whether they prescribed what reading was to be done at home. The majority prescribed home reading, most usually in the form of preparation for next day's reading lesson. The frequencies of teachers' practices are given in Table 2.18.

Table 2.18: Homework involving reading

Homework	P4	P5	P6	:	P7
Regular	61	54	49	:	41
Reading prescribed	(41)	(52)	(45)	:	(23)
Reading not prescribed	(20)	(2)	(4)	:	(18)
Occasional	18	11	19	:	20
None	19	37	38	:	32
All	98	102	106	:	93

All that emerges from the above table is a reduction in the frequency of regular homework over the P4 to P7 classes, but this is not accompanied by a corresponding decrease in the number of classes being given prescribed reading for homework. Interpretation is difficult, as there is a change in emphasis from reading as a basic skill in the younger classes to more functional reading in the older classes. Also, in their visits to schools, members of the Unit sensed even within the four year period of the inquiry, a drift in teachers' attitudes and practice towards less formal approaches to reading and studies generally. This, however, is an impression that is not easy to support with firm evidence.

The value of homework was a matter on which teachers held different opinions. Some gave homework to reinforce by exercises the work taught during the day, and others used it to stimulate and extend the pupils' interests. Others refrained from giving homework on the grounds that enough work could be done during the school day, and others because there was little prospect of its being done adequately at home. The 'class histories' for the three years P4, P5 and P6 show 16 classes receiving regular homework for all three years and 11 classes not

receiving it for any of the three years. For reading attainment in
P7, the A B C classification, the differences between the two sets of
classes are in Tables 2:19 and 2:20.

Table 2.19: Homework and P7 (reading attainment)

Homework	A	B	C	Total
All regular	2	5	9	16
No regular	2	8	1	11

For progress in reading between P4 and P7, the corresponding
figures are:

Table 2.20: Homework and P4 – 7 reading progress

Homework	A	B	C	Total
All regular	2	11	3	16
No regular	1	5	5	11

The two tables above do not point in the same direction, but both
could result from chance effects. There is a trend in the P7 reading
attainment tables for regular reading homework to be associated with
poorer performance; possibly because the poorer classes were thought
to need it more. The progress tables show an opposite trend. There is
no clear case established either for or against homework involving
reading.

Comparison of teachers' aims in teaching reading, and their views
on good and poor readers shows no relationship with their practice
regarding homework. Nor is there a relationship between homework
and the teachers' estimates of the extent of home encouragement in their
classes. The data are in Table 2.21.

Table 2.21: Homework and home encouragement (percentages)

Homework: Incidence of home encouragement in Classes P4, P5, P6, P7

	All or most	About Half	Few or None	Total
All regular	30	21	49	100%
No regular	28	19	53	100%

In common with previous findings, it appears that differences in teachers' opinions are not associated with differences in their practices.

Discussion and conclusions

This chapter has been confined to the teaching of the core aspect of reading in schools. Functional and recreational reading are discussed later, but when teachers talk of teaching reading it is this literary/comprehension type of reading that they refer to. The Bullock Committee (p. 521 of *A Language for Life*) finds 'There is no one method, medium, device or philosophy that holds the key to the process of learning to read.' Together with the finding of Professor Thorndike quoted at the head of this chapter, it is not surprising that the investigation into teaching of the main stream of reading in Scottish schools should reach a similar conclusion. None of the conditions, such as class size, or the philosophies, such as the aims of teaching reading, or the practices, such as oral reading or homework, show any consistent or significant relationship with differences in the reading achievement of primary school classes.

Perhaps this is a disappointing conclusion, as there is always the hope that systematic research investigation will reveal some pattern of practice that is clearly more successful than others, and reveal some combination of policy and method that will guide teachers along the road to successful teaching of reading. But it seems as if no such combination is there, and as the Bullock report says, there is no royal road.

In interpreting the findings of this report and others on similar educational topics, the methods of inquiry cannot be ignored. An inquiry into teaching practices at one stage in the pupils' progress can lead to certain conclusions and a similar inquiry at a different stage can lead to similar conclusions, either corroborating the first set of findings, or showing changes in emphasis or practices between older and younger pupils. Much but not all of the data in this chapter has been presented in this way. For example in Table 2.18 there appears a progressive diminution of the amount of regular homework given to classes P4, P5 and P6, from approximately 62 per cent to 50 per cent. These figures represent the practices of the teachers of those classes. But it does not follow that 50 per cent or more of the pupils progressing through these classes are being given regular homework, and therefore constitute a homogeneous group. In fact, only 16 of the 100 or so primary classes progressing from P4 to the end of P6, were being given regular homework. The remaining 85 per cent or so were subject during the three years to different practices, usually by different teachers.

With this in mind, a set of 'class histories' covering the P4, P5 and P6 years were constructed beginning with each P4 class, in which the different views and practices of the successive teachers of the class were recorded. To answer the question whether regular homework was associated with greater reading progress, only the data from 16 classes could be used for regular homework; the 11 classes in Table 2.20 given as 'No regular homework' contained only one class consistently receiving occasional homework, and no classes consistently receiving no homework. The question about regular homework could therefore only be answered by a comparison of 16 classes receiving regular homework with one class receiving occasional homework. Similarly, a comparison over three years of homework with no homework is impossible.

The same situation arises with other variables, as Table 2.22 shows. The numbers are of those classes where the variable is consistent for the class during its three years from P4 to P6.

Table 2.22: Class consistency from P4 to P6

	No. Classes
Teachers' experience	
Less than 2 years	0
2–5 years	3
More than 5 years	12
Homework	
Regular	16
Occasional	1
None	0
Teachers' aims for reading	
Interest/Enjoyment	8
Comprehension	0
Skills	0
Practical/Vocational	0
Oral reading (pupil)	
Regular	60
Occasional	2
None	0

The purpose of presenting these data is two-fold. One is to warn against too ready acceptance of findings based on one cross section of a school population. How the pupils are taught in one year may no be how they were taught in the preceding or following years. The other purpose is to offer the data as part explanation why classroom practices show no clear relationship with reading attainment or progress. The pupils are in fact subject to a very mixed set of teachers and practices during their years in the upper primary classes, and consistency is very much the exception. For example, of the 16 classes receiving regular homework consistently, seven had teachers of consistently the same experience, four of more than five years, two of two to five years, and one of less than two years. In the smaller schools it was often the same teacher. The result is that clear and consistent differences do not emerge, as they are not there as far as the pupils' experiences are concerned. This, however, is only a part explanation of the absence of clear relationship between teaching and learning to read. Other investigations, such as that quoted at the head of this chapter, and the Bullock report, both using methods other than those used here, reach the same conclusion. There appears to be no current system of methods of teaching reading which can be shown as superior to any other.

Perhaps, however, the conclusion is not wholly negative. The positive side of it is that the findings demonstrate no need for those involved in primary education to be unduly concerned with differences between the various practices commonly in use. The teachers may gain some confidence from this inquiry that the methods, organizations and practices prevailing in the upper primary classes are of much the same level of effectiveness. The moral for teachers is that they continue as they have been doing, but perhaps try to do it a little better. The evidence suggests that a more equitable distribution of special attention between good and poor readers may contribute to an overall improvement in average reading standards.

How much room for improvement is there? Despite some publicly expressed concern about decline in reading standards and rising illiteracy, this investigation gives no grounds for alarm or despondency about the standard of primary school reading within Scotland. Scottish primary 7 pupils are of virtually the same reading standard as their English contemporaries, and over the years 1972 to 1975 there has been an insignificant rise in primary 7 reading attainment, and certainly no fall.

There is no accepted and practicable definition of illiteracy. A reading age of nine years is often mentioned, but this seems very artificial. The average pupil entering P5, as judged by the test scores and the class readers used, can read, though not always fluently and not all kinds of material. But they are not illiterate in any non-technical sense of the word. This lack of definition raises difficulties in assessing the amount of illiteracy. The structure of the Edinburgh Reading tests prevents estimates of reading age outwith age ranges appropriate for the tests. Reading quotients are not suitable either. The lowest quotient is RQ70, but as the definition of RQ70 is that it separates the poorest 2·5 per cent of the pupils from the rest of their contemporaries the incidence of pupils below 70 RQ is predetermined.

An arbitrary decision was taken to regard as illiterate those pupils who scored fewer than 20 marks on the reading test, in which the maximum mark was 167 and the P7 mean score was 84. No pupils scored fewer than 10 marks, so the pupils defined here as 'illiterate' were not wholly unable to read. In P7 in 1972 there were 22 'illiterate' pupils, or 0·9 per cent, and in 1975 there were 20 'illiterate' pupils, or 0·8 per cent. Of the 42 pupils, 26 were boys and 16 were girls. These figures refer to pupils in attendance and completing the test, so may be a slight underestimate. But even allowing for this, the proportion of pupils defined as 'illiterate' cannot be far from one per cent, which may or may not be an acceptable proportion in a school population of a wide range of natural ability. It does seem that if there is a high incidence of illiteracy in Scotland, it is not at the end of primary schooling.

Chapter 3

Reading Books in School

'Of making many books there is no end, and much study
is a weariness of the flesh.'   *Ecclesiastes*

The primary school teachers draw upon four main types of reading
material in the P4 to P7 stages. The most frequent is the class reader,
followed in frequency by use of various 'Reading Laboratories', SRA and
Ward Lock being the most favoured. Another type is the less structured
material to be found in various paper backs, Puffin books and continuous
fiction. Finally there is the supplementary use of reading material from
class and school libraries, which is encouraged but not systematically
taught. Practices vary widely, but with few exceptions class readers
remain the mainstay in the teaching of reading.

Primary class readers

A list of the most commonly used series of class readers is appended
to this chapter, where it will be observed that in the majority of them
different books are being used throughout the P4 to P7 span. The use
made of them by teachers is shown in Table 3.1

Table 3.1: Use of class readers (P4 to P7)

Class	None	One	Several	No. Classes
P4	1	21	77	99
P5	2	15	82	99
P6	4	17	87	108
P7	6	29	62	97

Those entered as 'None' are classes using continuous fiction or
shorter booklets of the Puffin type as the main source of reading
material, supplemented usually by reading laboratories. The entries

under 'One' are those classes where only one class reader is used at any given time. These classes include about six or so small schools, where the number of pupils in a class may be very small, as well as four larger classes whose teachers considered the class level of attainment to be very uniform. In the 'Several' entries the practice of having pupils at different stages of reading progress reading different books in the same series, and that of having pupils reading books of roughly the same level, but from different series, were about equally common.

It is evident that the practice of working through a class reader with all pupils has virtually disappeared from these Scottish primary schools and the main feature is variety rather than uniformity. With a few exceptions, class teachers did not express serious dissatisfaction with the resources available to them. Some of the series used are perhaps rather elderly, and do not reflect current views on racial and sexual integration. Apart from the fact that in the sample investigated the number of immigrant children, except those from other parts of the British Isles, is very small indeed, this investigation has no evidence to offer, and therefore no comment to make.

Reading laboratories

These are becoming more frequently used in primary school classes. In P4, 48 per cent of the classes use one, in P5, 66 per cent, in P6, 77 per cent, and in P7 (session 1972/3) 43 per cent. The Table 3:2 gives the data.

From the Table, it appears that the SRA series is the most frequently used. The arrangements for use of reading laboratories are most commonly that the material is circulated round the teachers of the appropriate classes, and each teacher has the material for one term. During this time, the teachers often tend to dispense with the class reader, and where this occurs, the class is recorded below as 'Sole' use. The other common practice is for the material to be used as supplementary to the class reader for a longer period. Where teachers expressed a definite opinion of its value, this was recorded. The remaining teachers had no definite views. Not unexpectedly, the majority of users held a favourable opinion of the language laboratories; where there is choice, it is less likely that those holding unfavourable opinions would be using the material. Decisions by head teachers and class teachers on the use of reading laboratories are not wholly determined on educational grounds; there is an element of expense. Nevertheless, there appears an increasing use of reading laboratories as a method of teaching reading.

Table 3.2: Use of reading laboratories

Class P4 (1972–3)	No. Using	Supplementary	Sole	Duration of Use (terms)			Teachers' Views	
				1	2	3	Fav.	Unfav.
SRA	40	40	0	16	11	4	18	4
Ward Lock	6	6	0	3	2	0	1	0
None	49							
P5 (1973–4)								
SRA	63	47	16	34	14	15	48	7
Ward Lock	3	3	0	2	0	1	0	1
None	35							
P6 (1974–5)								
SRA	72	43	29	42	18	7	52	6
Ward Lock	9	4	4	5	2	1	8	0
None	24							
P7 (1972–3)								
SRA	38	32	3	9	2	8	3	4
Ward Lock	4	4	0	2	0	1	0	1
None	55							

The plan of this investigation did not envisage an experimental inquiry into the effectiveness of reading laboratories, either as the sole medium of teaching reading, or supplementary to class readers or supplemented by other reading resources. This would require an experimental approach devised for the purpose, with prescribed use of Reading Laboratories by teachers, and control groups where they were not used. In the primary classes in this investigation there were five who recorded no use of reading laboratories between P4 and P7, and 23 who used them in all three years. There was no significant difference in reading attainment and progress between the two groups.

Secondary school readers

The teaching of reading as such in the secondary schools was virtually confined to the English and remedial departments. In the English teaching, very little use was made of the kind of class reader used in primary classes; the tendency in some upper primary classes to use continuous prose, mostly novels, became the general practice in the secondary classes. Much the same applied in the remedial classes. The variety of books used rendered classification of little value, but modern prose fiction of the *Catcher in the Rye* type predominated. The teaching emphasis was much more on content and comprehension than reading skill, apart from some remedial pupils.

Readability

Assessing the readability of written material is essentially the determining of how far the material read is appropriate for the reading ability of the reader. Generally, fluency of reading and amount of comprehension are the criteria. A short but comprehensive discussion is given by Gilliland*. There are various formulae for assessing readability, American in origin, and which express readability level in terms of an index which can be converted to American school grades. Conversion to Scottish or English school classes is therefore only approximate.

Of the several readability formulae available, the one called SMOG was used. This formula, devised by McLaughlin in 1969, operates as follows: Take a sample of ten consecutive sentences near the beginning, another sample of ten near the middle, and a third sample near the end of the reading material being assessed. In these 30 sentences every word of three or more syllables is counted each time it occurs. Take the square root of this number of words, and add three. This gives the SMOG index. It is obvious that this is a very rough and ready method of assessment of readability, but there is no evidence that more sophisticated methods are significantly superior to the extent of justifying the much more lengthy and complicated methods of computation involved. Several passages from primary class readers were assessed by other formulae, the Flesch and the Dale-Chall as well as the SMOG. The order of difficulty was the same for all three formulae, though the intervals of difficulty were not the same. The equation of readability index to school grade varied, as some formulae assessed complete comprehension, others average comprehension, but again there was agreement on rank order of readability. As SMOG was the simplest and most economical to operate, it has been adopted here.

This formula was applied to the most commonly used class reader series, and the data are appended to this chapter. To obtain some sort of equivalence between SMOG index and primary school class, the formula was applied to Edinburgh Reading Test Stages 2 and 3. Though this application of SMOG to reading tests may not be entirely correct, it appears to be the best means of making a rough assessment. Stage 2 gave a SMOG index of 4. The median age for reading quotient 100 is 9 years 6 months, which gives a primary 5 class. For Stage 3, the SMOG index was 6, which gives an age of 11 years 4 months, that is P7. For the

---

*GILLILAND, J. (1972), *Readability*, UKRA. University of London Press, London.

average pupil, the class in primary school appears to be SMOG index plus one. Assuming this to be valid, the SMOG index alone would roughly indicate the primary class in which most pupils would be able to comprehend the reading material, the SMOG index plus one, the primary class in which the average pupil could comprehend, and SMOG index plus two, the class in which the better readers only could be expected to comprehend the material. This is very clearly a coarse measure of the suitability of reading material for different classes, but as both the reading ability of pupils within classes and the level of content within readers varies considerably, a coarse estimate is all that can be expected.

The readability index for any given reader is an average, which does not exclude occasional easier or more difficult passages appearing from time to time. In the appended tables, the indices recorded were those from two or more samples of 30 sentences, so they are a little more reliable than a single SMOG index. There are occasional minor fluctuations in the grading, but the graded series listed do show progression from one grade to the next, and in some, *New Worlds to Conquer* for example, the grading is much steeper than in others.

For P6, the most frequently used single reading books are in Table 3.3 together with the SMOG index:

Table 3.3: Most frequently recorded P6 reader, with SMOG Index

Reader	Book	SMOG
McIver First Aid	D	6
Wide Range	6	4·5
New Worlds to Conquer	4	7·5
Swift	4	4
Good Company	4	6
Enjoy Reading	4	5
SRA Lab + Pilot Library	IIC	7·5

A similar table for other classes and books can be made from the data in the appended tables. The readability index depends on sample passages from the books, so there is some sampling unreliability in the index values; it is unlikely, however, that this unreliability is sufficient to account for the considerable difference in average readability of the class readers used, so it would appear that the reading tasks set to P6 pupils vary in difficulty. There is no significant relationship between books used and class reading progress or attainment, but it must be kept in mind that classes using only one reader as the sole medium of teaching reading are very much in the minority.

Conclusions

The survey indicates that the class reader series is still the most common vehicle for the teaching of reading to primary school pupils. The older practice of having one reader per class, which was systematically worked through, has disappeared from primary schools. The prevailing practice is towards greater flexibility in the use of class readers, with an increasing tendency to supplement the class readers by Reading Laboratories, which began as an aid to backward readers, but which have developed into a general teaching device. Research findings on the earlier uses of Reading Laboratories tended to confirm their remedial function, in that the poorer readers showed greater relative progress than the better readers when these Laboratories were used. But the more recent development as a teaching aid for all pupils still awaits investigation, and no firm conclusions can be reached on their efficacy at present. The other practice in the upper primary classes, of replacing class readers by continuous reading, mainly of novels, is not as yet widespread, but does have the possible merit of introducing primary pupils to secondary school practice. The main impression given is increasing flexibility in the use of different kinds of reading material available.

The search for a precise and objective method of assessing readability of material has a long history, but success is only partial. The need for caution in interpreting readability indices has been mentioned, but partial progress does not mean failure. The SMOG indices used here do agree with the established grading of books in series, and should give some guidance to the teacher in the selection of appropriate books for more and less advanced readers in the class, and to a teacher seeking a relatively easy book to encourage fluency or a more difficult reading task for the pupils to master.

Appendix

Table 3.1A: Frequency of use of class readers (P4 to P7)

(*Signifies most frequently mentioned in series per class)

Series						Number of mentions			
(*either one or more of*)						P4	P5	P6 :	P7
McIver First Aid									
A	B*	C				46			
A	B	C*	D	E			51		
B	C	D*	E	F				45	
A	B	C	D	E*	F				45

Series	P4	P5	P6	:	P7
Wide Range					
1–5 (3*)	35				
1–6 (4* 5*)		27			
3 4 5 6*			20		
4 5* 6					11
New Worlds to Conquer					
1 2	25				
1 2* 3 4		20			
1 2 3 4* 5			28		
4 5					15
Swift					
1 2	18				
1 3		10			
2 3 4* 5			22		
4 5					13
Good Company					
1 2 3	12				
1 2* 3* 4 5		14			
2 4* 5 6			16		
2 3 5 6					6
Enjoy Reading					
2	11				
1 2 3*		14			
1 2 3 4* 5			22		
5					5
Ladybird					
2 3 4 6* 7* 8 12	18	10	3		1
Janet & John ⎫	14				
Happy Venture ⎬		7			
Treasure Trail ⎭			3		
—					0
Griffin ⎫	0				
Ideal ⎬		7			
New Ideal ⎭			9		
Essential					22
Fiction (paperback Puffin, etc.)	0	10	6		11
Number of classes	99	99	108		97

Table 3.2A: Primary class reader series: SMOG readability index

McIver First Aid Readers (Gibson)	SMOG Index		Swift Readers (Harrap)	SMOG Index
A	4		1	3
B	4		2	3·5
C	5·5		3	3·5
D	6·0		4	4
E	6·0		5	6
F	6·0			

Wide Range Readers (Oliver & Boyd)			New Worlds to Conquer (Chambers)	
1. Blue		4	1	4
1. Green	3·5		2	4·5
			3	6
2. Blue		2·5	4	7·5
2. Green	4		5	8
3. Blue		3		
3. Green	4·5			
4. Blue		4		
4. Green	5			
5. Blue		3		
5. Green	3·5			
6. Blue		5		
6. Green	4·5			

Enjoy Reading (Chambers)		Good Company (Johnston & Bacon)	
1	4	1	3·5
2	3	2	4·5
3	6	3	5
4	6	4	6
5	6	5	5·5
		6	6

Chapter 4

Functional Reading

'Insofar as anything done under or for the purpose of a regulation revoked by these regulations and in force at the coming into operation of these regulations could have been done under or for the purposes of a provision of these regulations, it shall continue in force and be deemed to have been done under or for the purposes of that provision'.

Statutory Instruments 1975 No. 1135 (S176)
Education (Scotland)

The notion of a literate democracy is one which developed during last century, and became effective in the 1870s in Britain with the introduction of general compulsory education. With increasing complexity of governmental activity, and greater bureaucratic intervention in both the private and occupational life of the citizens, it is becoming increasingly doubtful if a basic literacy continues to be adequate. There have been few inquiries into the reading skills involved in different occupations, but it is probable that there is an increasing number in which reading is required as a necessary occupational skill. A Canadian study* of 37 occupations (rural and urban) showed 90 per cent of the occupations required 'reading comprehension', 54 per cent required 'interpretative' reading, and 11 per cent 'evaluative' reading. All involved some reading and filling in of forms, and 97 per cent involved some use of books or manuals, usually only occasionally.

Though the development of such occupational reading skills may be considered as part of the duty of the secondary schools, even within schools the reading requirements of the various studies appear to be increasing in range and complexity. In both primary and secondary schools

*A. D. Smith, Department of Manpower and Immigration, Prince Albert, Saskatchewan, Canada.

the practice of direct class teaching is being replaced by greater emphasis on individual or group study by the pupils, which frequently involves reading as an integral part of such study. This reading is what is here called functional reading. It is doubtful, however, if this extension of learning methods has been accompanied by corresponding guidance and practice in the different reading skills required for effective study. It is perhaps significant that though nearly all primary teachers use some kind of 'project' approach, virtually none of them depend on it in the teaching of reading, writing or arithmetic. There the teachers seem to rely on the more established methods with whose techniques they are more familiar.

Reading in primary school mathematics

The functional reading in primary classes is of two types. There is the reading required for the study of texts used for subjects other than English or language, and the study required for 'projects' where specific texts were not used. The only subject where texts were almost uniformly used was mathematics, and in the very few classes where books were not used, there were sets of work cards, either published or prepared by the teacher. The teachers followed for maths the same general practice as with class readers, using more than one text according to the needs of their pupils. In the P4 to P7 classes 747 mentions of maths books or cards were made for 354 classes, giving an average of 2·1 books per class. The most frequently used maths texts are given in Appendix Table I at the end of this chapter. As this investigation concerns reading, two aspects of the maths books were examined. Many teachers reported that pupils had difficulty not only with the maths content of the books, but reading difficulties as well. Analyses showed that the percentage of teachers reporting some reading difficulty with these texts was P4, 30 per cent, P5, 28 per cent, P6, 12 per cent and P7, 28 per cent. Why P6 is an exception is not clear. It is the most frequently used texts that attract the highest incidence of reports about reading difficulties. The total incidence for P4 to P7, expressed as percentages of number of mentions, is as follows: Making Sure of Maths 24 per cent, Alpha 29 per cent, Beta 31 per cent, Work Cards seven per cent and others 15 per cent. To ascertain whether there was any objective basis for the teachers' opinions, a rough and ready index of readability was obtained for the most frequently used series. The SMOG index was used, as for class reader series. These texts constitute 66 per cent of all textbooks mentioned. When these indices are compared with those given in the previous chapter on class readers, there is on average very little difference. There is more dif-

Table 4.1: Readability (SMOG) of mathematics textbooks

Text	1	2	3	4	5
			Books in Series		
Making Sure of Maths	3·5	3·5	4	5	5
Metric Maths	3·5	3·5	5	5	–
Alpha Maths	5	5	5·5	6·5	6
Beta Maths	4·5	4·5	5	5	–

ference in the grading of the books in the series, in that the difference between the first and the later books in the maths series is less than that in the readers. Why the teachers reported reading difficulties to an extent of more than a quarter of all reports can be inferred from interviews with class teachers. The teachers' expectations tended to be that the teaching of maths should not be impeded by purely reading difficulties. This is reasonable enough, but there appear to be no commonly used 'modern' maths books which are expressed in language clearly below that of the average pupil. The result is that poorer readers may have a double difficulty. The main criticism of the reading aspect of the maths books was difficult vocabulary and too concise and precise sentence structure. This would suggest that a different style of reading skill may be required for maths text as compared with class readers, but there was little evidence that teachers took positive steps to meet this reading requirement. A small number of teachers (17 per cent in P4, two per cent in P5, three per cent in P6 and four per cent in P7) reported grading the maths books according to reading competence of their pupils, but this tended to be regarded by them as an unsatisfactory if necessary practice. Also, about half of the teachers using work cards gave reading difficulties as one of the reasons for preferring them to textbooks.

The finding that over a quarter of the teachers reported reading difficulties with mathematics textbooks is one that cannot be ignored. The incidence of complaints is not related to the average reading attainment of their classes, and represents a substantial number of pupils whose progress in learning mathematics is impeded by reading difficulties. The solution suggested is twofold. The reading requirements in mathematics books could be more carefully examined before publication, and teachers could adopt a more direct approach to the teaching of the necessary reading skills for such studies, regarding the teaching of such skills as an integral part of this method of teaching mathematics. This is one instance of the comparative neglect of the functional aspects of reading in schools, and it appears from the teachers' reports that to rely on the skills taught as 'Reading' in primary classes as adequate for the reading requirements in other studies is not sufficient.

Reading in other primary subjects

It was the exception rather than the rule to find teachers using textbooks in science, history or geography as a regular practice. Over P4, P5, P6 and P7, only 49 mentions were made of science texts, and 23 of prepared work cards. Only two teachers, both in P4, mentioned reading difficulties, though the readability level of these texts was very similar to that of the mathematics text. The probable explanation is that the grant-aided schools were the most frequent users of class textbooks in science. In history teaching, a fairly constant 30 classes in each year reported use of history textbooks, with about 37 mentions of books per year. Again, little reading difficulty was reported, though the SMOG index of the more popular books tended to be fairly high. The two most used texts were 'Living History' (McDougall) (Book 2 SMOG=4, Book 4 SMOG=7), and Chambers' Scottish History (Book 3 SMOG=6). For geography books, the situation is very similar, P4 giving 37 mentions, P5, 18 mentions, P6, 10 mentions and P7, 28 mentions. The decrease from P4 to P6 may represent a diminishing tendency to use class texts in geography, which does not appear for history. Again, there is very little mention of reading difficulties, and a wide variety of textbooks are used (there are no clear favourites) showed that they appeared to be easier reading than the history texts.

Apart from an increasing use of workcards as the pupils moved to the higher primary classes, the use of textbooks was not a major element in the teaching of the subject areas investigated. In contrast to the mathematics texts, the science, history and geography texts were written in much the same style of continuous prose as the class readers, which may account for the less frequent reports of reading difficulties.

Reading in projects

Not all the classes using textbooks depended on them as the sole means of teaching. The most favoured practice for teaching other than English and mathematics was projects, sometimes supplemented by use of texts. The term project is used here for activities variously described as topics, assignments, individual or group study as well as projects. The data obtained on the use of projects are given in Table 4.2.

The topics for the projects varied widely, including such as Fish, EEC, Transport, Chocolate, Edinburgh, Pirates and Costume. As the

Table 4.2: Reading in project studies

	Number of Classes				Total
	P4	P5	P6	P7	
1. No. classes using projects	93	89	97	82	361
No. classes not using projects	4	8	10	14	36
2. Reading required for projects:					
A lot	24	22	36	28	110
Some	28	18	55	27	128
Little or none	17	12	5	2	36
3. Reading graded to pupils' ability:					
Yes	57	41	52	52	202
No	18	36	44	15	113
4. Main sources of reading:					
School/class library books	45	82	82	33	242
Pupils' own books	7	16	12	6	41
Work cards	8	8	17	4	37
Leaflets, etc.	8	10	8	4	30

table shows, the main source of reading material is library books, frequently reference books. Though the majority of the teachers reported grading reading requirements according to pupils' abilities, the general practice did not include close supervision of pupils' reading, and it appeared that frequently the interested and able pupils read widely on a topic while the poorest readers did little other than copy short statements or cut out pictures. Some teachers gave *ad hoc* help to pupils in the use of reference books, but there appeared little systematic guidance given to pupils on the reading and study techniques required to make the most effective use of their time and efforts. In view of the widespread use of project methods, where over 90 per cent of the classes employed them, and of these about 60 per cent used them as the main method of teaching outside the three Rs, it again seems that teachers are tending to set pupils reading tasks without giving them adequate guidance and practice on how to perform these tasks efficiently.

Reading styles in secondary schools

In view of the situation discussed above, a list of reading styles which seemed appropriate for the functional reading requirements in primary and secondary schools was compiled and submitted during personal interviews to 152 P6 and P7 teachers and to 180 secondary teachers of English, history and related subjects, mathematics, science (mainly chemistry), technical and domestic. The list of reading styles or skills was a composite drawn from various sources and was compiled after discussions with a number of class teachers, about the nature of the reading required from their pupils. The six styles selected were:

1. Rapid reading for gist of passage;
2. Rapid reading for specified information;
3. Rapid reading for relevant information;
4. Detailed reading to follow instructions;
5. Detailed reading to follow argument;
6. Reading for appreciation of style.

The styles numbered 2 and 3 were distinguished between by most teachers, but a few reported that they did not consider the distinction a necessary one. The difference intended was that specified information meant that the reader knew the question to be answered, e.g. 'What was the first steamship to cross the Atlantic?', whereas relevant information meant that the reader was to find out as much as possible about whales for example.

The primary teachers classified the degree of emphasis given to the different styles as 'A lot', 'Some' or 'Little or None'. The responses are given as percentages in Table 4.3.

Table 4.3: Reading styles on P6 and P7 classes

| | *Style (as listed in text)* | | | | | | |
	1	*2*	*3*	*4*	*5*	*6*	*All*
A lot	28	43	60	55	4	6	33
Little or None	20	11	3	4	84	63	31

The main emphasis in the primary school is on rapid reading for relevant information and on detailed reading to follow instructions. Most teachers commented that reading to follow an argument required a maturity that their pupils did not have. Reading for literary style played a small part in primary practice.

In the secondary schools reading requirements varied according to subject area. Details of the responses are given in Appendix Table II to this chapter.

There is a reasonable, but not exact correspondence between secondary requirements and primary emphasis. In both, rapid reading for relevant information and detailed reading to follow instructions are the most frequent, but secondary demands are clearly greater for detailed reading to follow instructions, and this is where the secondary teachers are least satisfied with the pupils' competence. In contrast, the secondary teachers are most satisfied with rapid reading for relevant information, which is the style most emphasized by the primary teachers. How the general figure of 44 per cent of secondary teachers satisfied with their pupils' level of competence for first and second year secondary studies is to be interpreted is doubtful. It is unrealistic to expect teachers at a later stage to be wholly satisfied with the products of the teachers of the earlier stages, but 44 per cent does seem a rather low level of satisfactoriness. Among the secondary school subject areas, the technical subjects teachers are least demanding of a range of reading skills, but within their limited requirements are most satisfied with their pupils' competence. The teachers of English require the widest range of reading styles, and appear as the most satisfied customers of the primary school products. The suspicion is that the primary teachers are more involved with the literary emphasis required by the teachers of English than with the much wider range of more functional needs of the other secondary school subjects.

A fuller discussion of secondary school practices follows in a later chapter.

Appendix

Table 4.1A: Frequency of use of maths/arith textbooks

Text	No. of Mentions				Mention of Reading Difficulties			
	P4	P5	P6 :	P7	P4	P5	P6 :	P7
Making Sure of Maths (Holmes McDougall)	43	50	72	42	12	22	11	17
Metric Maths (Holmes McDougall)	21	26	29	22	9	6	2	7
Alpha Maths (Schofield & Sims)	19	17	12	10	9	6	0	2
Beta Maths (Schofield & Sims)	32	44	37	19	14	16	7	4
Work Cards (Various)	16	16	14	11	2	1	0	1
Others	34	48	56	37	4	5	9	8
All	165	201	240	141	50	56	29	39
No. Classes	86	98	101	69	36	42	27	25

Table 4.2A: Reading style requirements (S1 and S2 teachers' responses)

Style	English (n=36) Des.	Pract.	% Satis.	History (n=33) Des.	Pract.	% Satis.	Maths (n=31) Des.	Pract.	% Satis.
1	31	19	61	22	10	45	3	3	100
2	28	16	57	25	12	48	6	2	33
3	31	19	61	32	18	56	10	6	60
4	33	27	82	29	15	52	31	18	58
5	22	12	55	18	4	22	13	4	31
6	30	14	47	5	2	40	0	0	—
All	175	107	61%	131	61	47%	63	33	52%

Style	Science (n=30) Des.	Pract.	% Satis.	Technical (n=24) Des.	Pract.	% Satis.	Domestic (n=26) Des.	Pract.	% Satis.
1	7	1	14	1	0	0	5	1	20
2	13	2	15	3	3	100	4	0	0
3	13	6	46	3	2	67	9	5	56
4	28	12	43	22	14	64	25	14	56
5	13	5	38	0	0	—	2	0	0
6	0	0	—	0	0	—	0	0	—
All	74	26	35%	29	19	66%	45	20	44%

Style	Remedial (n=20) Des.	Pract.	% Satis.	All (less Remedial) (n=180) Des.	Pract.	% Satis.
1	12	5	42	69	34	49
2	10	3	30	79	35	44
3	15	7	47	98	56	57
4	18	12	67	164	60	37
5	8	0	0	67	25	37
6	8	0	0	35	16	46
All	71	27	38%	512	226	44%

Des.: Desirable.
Pract.: Practicable (i.e. pupils are sufficiently competent).
% Satis.: Percentages of teachers reporting pupils as sufficiently competent.

Reading Styles: 1. Rapid for gist.
　　　　　　　　2. Rapid for specified information.
　　　　　　　　3. Rapid for relevant information.
　　　　　　　　4. Detailed to follow instructions.
　　　　　　　　5. Detailed to follow argument.
　　　　　　　　6. Appreciation of style.

Chapter 5

Reading out of School

'All the land that lies between the two ends of the rainbow'
Sir Walter Scott, *The Heart of Midlothian.*

Each session at the end of May, all pupils were asked to complete a return on their reading out of school for a period of seven days. Class teachers gave such assistance as they considered necessary, but the pupils were free to enter what they had read or whether they had read nothing. Having been assured that the returns would not be marked, the pupils appear to have answered freely and honestly. It cannot be claimed that the returns represent a precise record; for one thing, they refer to a sample week only at a time of year when reading is probably not at its maximum, and for another, the thoroughness of reading cannot be assessed. As adults do not necessarily read books meticulously from cover to cover, nor newspapers from front to back page, it would be unreasonable to demand higher standards from school pupils. The word 'read', therefore, covers reading activities of various degrees of intensity.

The pupils recorded their reading under the following main headings:

(a) Books;
(b) Comics, newspapers, magazines;
(c) Sources of reading material – private, school, public library;
(d) Relation to school work – none, preparation for school reading following interest aroused in school.

The group (b) above is hereafter referred to as ephemera. The distinction between books and ephemera is two-fold. There is the difference in format and often price, and the difference that ephemera may appear daily as with newspapers, or weekly as with most comics or

monthly as with some magazines. The result is that the list of all
books read is so long and varied as to defy condensation, and even
regular favourites like *Black Beauty* and *Heidi* each represents less than
two per cent of the titles mentioned. The reader of books may read *Black
Beauty* once only, so the chances of its appearing frequently in one week's
reading record are small, whereas the regular reader of the *Beano* would
record it whatever sample week was chosen. The list of ephemera
therefore contains fewer titles than the list of books, but because they
are regularly available and take less time to read, there is a greater
frequency of ephemera recorded than books.

The Consumption of books

The incidence and development of book reading is given in Table 5.1.

Table 5.1: Book reading by class

Class	No. of books read	No. of readers	No. of non-readers	Per cent non-readers	Mean No. books per pupil	Mean No. books per reader
P4	3527	1719	792	32	1·4	2·1
P5	3912	1740	614	26	1·7	2·2
P6	4269	1739	571	25	1·8	2·5
P7	4082	2004	472	19	1·6	2·0
S1	4452	2100	638	23	1·6	2·1
S2	3606	1966	695	26	1·5	1·8

The maximum consumption of books is in P6, and though the increase in book reading up to P6 and P7 may be explained by increasing
fluency and widening interest, it is not clear why the amount of reading
in secondary school should diminish to something approaching P4 level.
Possibly a less readily available supply of books in school libraries
may have something to do with it. In a study for the Schools Council,
Whitehead reported finding secondary school libraries less well stocked
with fiction than primary school or class libraries, and books on humour
and sport were most lacking. Also it may be that what is read is read more
thoroughly by the older pupils. Nevertheless, it remains a disturbing
feature that after the completion of primary schooling the amount of
leisure reading of books should diminish rather than increase.

Of the 23,848 books recorded as read by the pupils, very few indeed
occur with any frequency, and the few recurring titles appear almost
equally throughout the range of classes. The variety of books is very
great, ranging from Whitfield's *Sermons* and Darwin's *Origin of Species*

to titles like *The Grinning Skull* and *Pam's Ponies*. Popular science and hobbies are more favoured by boys, and romance, Enid Blyton and ponies by girls. The outstanding feature is the extensiveness of range of titles and the preponderance of books of what on literary standards would be described as trashy, but which in contrast to the 'better quality' books, are read more frequently. Perhaps there is a moral here for school libraries.

Consumption of ephemera

During the sample week, all pupils read 61,295 newspapers, comics and magazines. The data by classes are in Table 5.2.

Table 5.2: Reading of ephemera by class

Class	No. of ephemera read	No. of readers	No. of non-readers	Per cent non-readers	No. of ephemera per reader
P4	6693	2162	349	14	3·1
P5	8826	2135	219	9	4·1
P6	10478	2148	162	7	4·9
P7	10186	2370	106	4	4·3
S1	13629	2607	131	5	5·2
S2	11483	2339	122	5	4·9

The reading of comics newspapers and magazines does not show the same decrease in secondary schools as is shown for book reading. From P6 onwards, the amount of ephemera read does not change to any considerable degree, and the distinction is between P4 and P5 and the later classes. The ratio of ephemera to books read increases steadily throughout the classes, the ratio rising from 1·9 in P4, through 2·3 in P5, 2·5 in P6, 2·5 in P7, 3·1 in S1, to 3·2 in S2. In short, the largest amount of book reading compared to ephemera is in P4, and the least in S2, where three times as much ephemera as books are read. The major source of ephemera is private, and the larger consumption by older pupils may only represent more pocket money. But this is not the only explanation.

Ephemera fall into three main groups. There are the daily and weekly national and local newspapers, about 40 per cent of all titles; the comics of different kinds, about another 40 per cent; and a miscellaneous list of periodicals and magazines dealing with matters ranging from angling to model construction, and beekeeping to dressmaking. Some are of a fairly high level of content and discussion. The newspapers closely represent the national pattern of circulation and appear to be those obtained for the family and not particularly for school pupils. In P7, for example, 18 per cent of the pupils recorded themselves as reading the *Daily Record*, 16 per cent the *Sunday Post*, 10 per cent the *Daily Express*, 7 per cent *The Scotsman*, and six per cent local newspapers. The majority reported more than one newspaper. The comics, whether read or not by the rest of the family, are produced for the school pupil reader and are a fairly easily identifiable group. Those listed in Table 5.3 are in order of frequency of mention by classes P4, P7 and S2, and each list accounts for more than 50 per cent of the readership of all comics.

Table 5.3: Comic reading by classes by sex

	Boys			Girls	
P4	P7	S2	P4	P7	S2
Beano	*Beano*	*Victor*	Dandy	*Jackie*	*Jackie*
Dandy	*Victor*	Wizard	*Diana*	Bunty	Mates
Victor	*Dandy*	Warlord	*Jackie*	Diana	*Diana*
Beezer	*Beezer*	Hotspur	Beano	Mandy	*Beano*
Marvel	Hotspur	*Beano*	Bunty	Music Star	Pink
Buzz	Marvel	*Dandy*	*Judy*	*Judy*	Fab 208
Shiver & Shake	Wizard	*Beezer*	Debbie	Debbie	*Bunty*
Topper	Sparky	Hornet		Pink	*Judy*
Sparky	Hornet		Mandy	Tammy	O.K.
				Beezer	
				Beano	

The most striking feature of the list is the large common element in the reading of the eight-year-olds, the eleven-year-olds and the thirteen-year-olds. The titles in italics are those which appear in the most popular reading for all three classes, and the *Beano* manages to appear in all lists. Also, though there are comics common to both boys and girls, there is no difficulty in recognizing which list is the boys' selection and which the girls'. There is a fairly sharp differentiation which is not so obvious in book reading.

As each list represents just more than half the comics read per week, the total reading of even the comics listed constitutes a very large proportion of the pupils' reading, possibly as much as is read within school. Very roughly allowing each pupil 1·5 books and four comics and newspapers per week, it is arguable that more reading is done per week outwith school than within school. It is likely that reading in school is done more slowly and meticulously, but the average pupil appears to do more to lay the foundations for recreational reading in later life outwith the classroom than within it. Whether it is the schools' duty to encourage and develop the reading of such material is debatable, but it must be kept in mind that such reading constitutes a very substantial part of the pupils' reading activity.

Nor is the level of reading competence required for ephemeral reading necessarily low. The SMOG readability index as far as it is appropriate for a selection of ephemera shows a fairly high level.

Table 5.4: SMOG Index of Selected Ephemera

SMOG Index	Titles
4	*Dandy, Beezer, Beano*
5	*Bunty, Music Star*
6·5	*Diana, Look-in*
7	*Jackie, Daily Express, Daily Record*
8	*Music Scene*
9	*Scotsman*

Of the most popular school readers, only *New Worlds to Conquer* (Bk 4 and 5) rate higher than *Diana, Look-in* or *Jackie*. None of the commonly-used maths books do. A study (in 1948) by Sister Jude of Notre Dame College in Glasgow showed that in strip comics only seven per cent of the words used were slang or not acceptable in school readers. Ninety-three per cent of the vocabulary was common to comics and school readers. The impression gained from the present investigation is that the often rather puerile content of much of the ephemera has tended to divert attention from both the reasonably high literacy level required of the reader, and the large part these ephemera play in the total reading of school children.

Out of school reading and reading attainment and progress

There are different ways of presenting the relationship between out-of-school reading and reading attainment and progress as measured by the reading tests. The differences between good and poor readers in the secondary and primary schools are discussed later in this report. The data relating the average amount of reading per school class to the reading attainment and progress of the classes are given in Table 5.5. The A B C classification is that previously used, and where the class progress is from P4 to P7, the reading progress is the difference between the average reading per class in P4 and P6. Similarly, the reading attainment in P7 is related to the average total consumption of reading material in the previous three years.

Table 5.5: Reading progress (P4 to P7) and increase in average consumption

	A	B	C
Average no. books	1·0	0·2	0·4
Average no. ephemera	2·4	1·9	1·4

Reading attainment (P7) with average consumption for preceding 3 years (P4, P5, P6)

	A	B	C
Average no. books	6·0	4·4	4·3
Average no. ephemera	12·1	10·4	9·7

There is a difference in pattern for books and ephemera. In book reading the A classes (the top quarter) are clearly ahead of the others, there being little difference between average and below average classes. Though the A classes read more ephemera than the others, there is not the same clear step between the A classes and the others as appears for books. It appears that reading of books is what distinguishes classes of higher reading standard from the others.

In secondary schools the great majority of classes were of mixed ability, so a similar grouping of classes would be meaningless. It is possible however to identify certain groups of classes. There are those called remedial, and those whose reading standard on the P7 test before entry to secondary school was above average (RQ of 105 or over). The relation between reading standard and out of school reading is even clearer, as is shown in Table 5.6. There are seven remedial and thirteen above average classes.

Table 5.6: Secondary class attainment and out of school reading

Class	Mean No. Books		Mean No. Ephemera	
	S1	S2	S1	S2
Remedial	0·8	1·0	2·8	3·5
Above average	2·3	2·7	4·6	5·3
All classes	1·6	1·5	5·0	4·7

The above average classes read about two and a half times as many books as the remedial classes, but only about the same amount of ephemera as all secondary classes. Once again, the distinction is in terms of books, the consumption of ephemera being more uniform among the different kinds of classes.

Non-readers of books and ephemera

A further presentation of the same topic can be made in terms of the proportion of pupils who report no reading during the sample week. The A B C classification here refers to the attainment of the class in the session that the returns were made. P6 is on the basis of the P5 reading test. Here the classes called 'S' are those of fewer than 10 pupils, predominantly in the smaller rural schools. Figures in Table 5.7 are percentages.

Table 5.7: Percentages of non-readers by class attainment

Class		Class Attainment				
		A	B	C	D	All
P4	Books	27	34	34	26	32
	Ephemera	9	14	20	4	14
P5	Books	21	27	31	21	26
	Ephemera	3	12	9	5	9
P6	Books	20	23	32	24	25
	Ephemera	6	7	7	0	7
P7	Books	9	22	24	13	19
	Ephemera	3	4	5	3	4
		Above Average		Remedial		All
S1	Books	8		42		23
	Ephemera	4		13		5
S2	Books	8		51		26
	Ephemera	3		15		5

As might be expected, the proportions of non-readers are generally similar to the pattern of average amount of reading. There are roughly about 25 per cent of pupils who report reading no books during the sample week, and about seven per cent who read no ephemera. Again, the S2 classes show a regression to about P5 level of consumption of books, though maintaining their reading of ephemera. The most notable features of the table are the relatively high level of readership in the smaller classes. Most are in rural schools, and more reading of ephemera in particular appears among them, though in fact their average level of reading attainment is not very high. The other feature is the very high, and increasing, incidence of non-readers in the two sets of remedial classes. By S2, half report no book reading and the proportion not reading ephemera is only exceeded by the poorer P4 classes. The inference is that in secondary schools an increasing number of the poorer readers appear to be abandoning the habit of reading altogether, even if it is for their own pleasure. Possibly the teachers' expectations of private reading are not so insistent as in primary classes. Most remedial class pupils should be able to read the *Beano*, *Victor* or *Dandy*, but appear to choose not to do so.

Sex differences in out of school reading

In the discussion of comics it was noted that the lists reported by boys were clearly distinguishable from those given by the girls. Also there appears a difference in the amount of reading done by boys and girls. For books, there is a fairly uniform difference from P4 to S2; the girls reading on average about 0·2 books per week more than the boys. Similarly, there is a fairly uniform eight per cent more non-readers among boys than among girls. For ephemera, the girls in P4, P5 and P6 read on average 0·3 fewer ephemera than boys, but from P7 to S2 the trend is reversed, the girls reading about 0·3 ephemera per week more than the boys. A similar reversal appears for proportion of non-readers, which is higher for boys in the earlier classes, but in the later classes the proportion of non-readers among boys steadily increases in comparison with the girls. The difference is however small, being of the order of one per cent more non-reading girls in P4 to P6, and three per cent more non-reading boys in P7 to S2. In general the girls, especially the older ones, read a little more than their male classmates.

Sources of out of school reading

For all kinds of reading outwith school, books and ephemera combined, about 90 per cent of pupils in all classes reported obtaining their reading material from private sources. These sources included the pupils' own purchases, and material obtained from family and friends. The incidence of private sources of reading was very constant throughout all classes from P4 to S2, and was not related to the reading attainment level of the classes. Even between the remedial and above average S1 and S2 classes, the difference was only of the order of 13 per cent, where 92 per cent of the above average and 79 per cent of the remedial pupils used private sources.

The public sources were classified either as within school (class library, school library or teacher) or outwith school (public library service). The dependence of public sources shows, unlike the private sources, changes according to class in school.

Table 5.8: Percentage of pupils using public sources

	Within School	*Outwith School*
P4	45	29
P5	35	28
P6	35	28
P7	27	24
S1	21	18
S2	17	14

The pupils up to P7 show a considerable dependence on school sources for their reading, which does not continue into the secondary school. Similarly, the use of the public library services drops between primary and secondary schools. There is also a general tendency in the P4 and P5 classes for the classes of lower reading attainment (the C classes) to make greatest use of school sources; in P6 and P7 it is the above average classes who make most use of school sources, while in secondary school there is no distinction between remedial and above average classes in their use of school sources.

The classes of higher average reading attainment throughout use the public library services to a greater extent than the others, the difference being most marked from P6 onwards. In secondary school, about 30 per cent of the pupils in above average classes use the public services, compared with 10 per cent of the remedial class pupils. The pupils in small classes record above average use of school sources, and below average for public sources, but as the rural school is often a distribution centre for the public services, it is possible that pupils may confuse the two sources.

Stimulation of out of school reading

Though there is some basis for satisfaction in that there does appear a substantial amount of out-of-school reading done by pupils, there is equally cause for concern in that whatever assessment is made, there appears a decrease in pupils' reading activities after P6 or P7.

The question arose whether the schools can and do stimulate interest which leads to reading by pupils outwith school. The pupils in each of the classes were asked whether their out of school reading was:

(a) preparing reading for school;
(b) looking up information for a project or other classwork;
(c) for pleasure about something which interested them in school;
(d) none of these.

The pupils could make more than one response, so the replies have been combined into three groups:

None [those answering (d)];
Preparation and/or Projects only [(a) and/or (b)];
Interest [any response to (c) whether with or without response to (a) or (b)].

Table 5.9 gives the percentages for boys and girls separately.

Table 5.9: Stimulation of out of school reading (percentages)

	None		Prep. and Projects only		Interests	
Class	B	G	B	G	B	G
P4	22	21	41	46	36	32
P5	35	32	51	53	30	28
P6	31	33	38	47	30	23
P7	41	39	32	39	26	22
S1	62	55	20	29	20	18
S2	60	56	21	29	18	15

The relation between school studies or any kind and out of school reading decreases almost threefold between P4 and S2, with only a small difference between boys and girls. What the rather conspicuous increase in leisure reading unrelated to school work in the secondary classes means is not clear. It may reflect a widening of the range of interests of the pupils, or it may reflect a reversion to less exacting reading by some pupils. Whatever the reason, the secondary pupils' reading has become more out of touch with school activities than has the primary pupils'. The amount of reading directly related to schoolwork also decreases between P4 and S2, though the girls appear a little more conscientious than the boys in this aspect of reading. The fact remains, however, that only about 25 per cent of the secondary pupils report any reading for their school studies, as compared with about 50 per cent in P5. As the inquiry was made in May, the figures may be an underestimate, but the trend from P4 to S2 is not likely to be affected. The amount of reading aroused by interest arising from school studies also shows a very marked diminution as the pupils move up the school, the amount in S2 being about half that in P4. In this the boys appear a little more responsive to school interest than the girls.

Conclusions and discussion

Though there is some reason for satisfaction in that the amount of reading done by pupils outwith school is considerable, about two books per reader per week, and more than four comics, newspapers and magazines, there are equally disturbing findings. There is about 25 per cent of the pupils who report reading no books during the sample week, and between five per cent and 10 per cent read no comics, magazines and newspapers. What is most disappointing is the way in which both the amount of book reading decreases after P6 and the lack of development in the bulk of the ephemera read. The comics read most frequently by primary and secondary pupils are substantially the same, and though there is an element of 'quality' ephemera, this is in the minority.

As is shown later, reading attainment and amount of out-of-school reading are positively related, especially in primary pupils, but what distinguishes the poorer from the better readers is the consumption of books rather than ephemera. It should also be pointed out that the decrease in average consumption of books in the secondary schools is not accompanied by a decline in reading attainment as assessed by the reading tests. A group of mainly poorer readers showed an almost uniform increase in test score between the beginning of P7 and the beginning of their S3 sessions. The most plausible explanation is that in the secondary classes the school reading requirements are maintaining, and to some extent developing, those components of reading ability assessed by the reading tests, but that they are not being reinforced by out of school reading as much in the secondary school as in the primary school.

Out-of-school reading related to, or stimulated by, school studies also declines very substantially as the pupils move up the school to S2, and this apparently is not compensated for by an extension of independent reading, as the use of public and school library sources also shows a marked decline in the upper classes. Only 17 per cent of S2 pupils use school sources, and 14 per cent use public library sources, as compared with 45 per cent and 29 per cent in P4. The whole picture is one of decline in, interest in, and habits of reading in top primary and lower secondary classes. The rot sets in after P6, and the only continuing reading is that of ephemera which are obtained from private sources by buying and borrowing. About 90 per cent of S2 pupils obtain their reading, mostly ephemera, from private sources, only about 15 per cent from school or public libraries. The reading of books and the use of libraries both decline in the secondary school.

How the situation is best remedied is not revealed by this inquiry. There are two possible lines of development indicated. One is greater interest in and stimulation of reading, however superficial, by the teachers in the secondary schools. Some is already done, but there appears room for a lot more. The other is development of the public and school library sources so as to supply a greater amount of the kind of reading preferred by the pupils. There is a suspicion that librarians tend to exercise a certain censorship in favour of 'better quality' reading matter. If this had the effect of directing pupils towards the reading of it, there would be no difficulty. But what appears to be happening is that pupils are having to face the choice of unpalatable reading or no reading, and many appear to opt for the latter. If adult illiteracy is as prevalent as it is claimed, it seems that the decline in literacy and reading habits may have its beginning in the early secondary school.

Chapter 6

The Teachers

> 'Learning teacheth more in one year than experience
> in twenty.' R. ASCHAM, *The Schoolmaster*.

It was no part of the investigation to assess the competence of
individual teachers in their teaching of reading. The intention was
rather to attempt to identify any characteristics of teachers, policies
or practices which appeared to be associated with better reading
achievement by the pupils. This in effect confines the investigation
to the primary schools, as the relationship between teachers and classes
in the secondary school is much less close and consistent. The secondary
pupils are taught by different teachers for different subjects, and not
all secondary pupils are taking the same courses. The relationships of
teachers to classes were too complicated to handle easily.

Primary teachers

The characteristics of the primary teachers, as obtained in personal
interviews with each teacher, are presented in Table 6.1A which appears
in the Appendix at the end of this chapter.

Teachers of less than six years' experience fill the majority of posts
in P4 classes, a little less than half in P5 and P6, but only a minority
in P7. As the category of more than 5 years includes all teachers with
six to forty or more years, it appears that most of the teaching done in
P4, P5 and P6 is by relatively less experienced teachers. The difference
in the P7 figures is due mainly to the custom in schools of giving P7
classes to more experienced teachers, and to the custom in the smaller
schools of head teachers with teaching duties taking P7 and to a lesser
extent P6 classes. This is also the main reason for the higher incidence
of graduates in P6 and P7.

Teachers' experience and class organization

During the period spanning teachers' experience, some forty years, a number of changes in educational attitudes and practices have taken place. One is a change from class to group teaching. It is interesting to see if the more experienced teachers continue to favour more traditional methods. Taking two groups of teachers, those with five years or less experience and those with more than five years, the relationship between class and group teaching is in Table 6.1. 'Any class' means that some class teaching is done, similarly with 'any group'. Classes P4 to P7 are combined.

Table 6.1: Teachers' experience by class and group teaching (percentages)

| | Teachers' Experience | | |
| | 5 years | More than | |
Class Organization	or less	5 years	Both
Any class	36	64	100
Any group	48	52	100
All teachers	41	59	100

There is some trend towards more use of class teaching and less of group teaching by the more experienced teachers. In fact, this trend is most marked in P4 and P6, but it does not reach the level of statistical significance. There is no clear evidence that more experienced teachers are not adapting to changing ideas about class organization.

It has already been shown that differences in class organization are not related to reading progress or attainment. Perhaps teachers' experience is. There are 25 classes which were taught throughout the P4 to P6 period by teachers with either five or fewer years of experience or with more than five years. The end results of their teaching of reading are given in Table 6.2.

Table 6.2: Teachers' experience of reading attainment and progress

| Teachers' Experience | P7 Attainment | | | P4-7 Progress | | |
	A	B	C	A	B	C
Five years or less	2	7	6	2	12	1
More than 5 years	2	8	0	1	7	2

The relationship is not clear cut. The classes of the more experienced teachers show slightly better attainment in P7, but less progress between P4 and P7. The differences are not significant statistically, and too much should not be read into them. It may possibly be that younger teachers are given less able classes.

Teachers' experience and practices

The relationship between teachers' experience and practices was examined to find out if the more experienced teachers differed significantly from the less experienced in their attitudes and practices. As far as aims of teaching reading are concerned the teachers' responses do not vary greatly by experience. Teachers of two years' or less experience give a pattern of responses similar to those of two to five years' and are included in the five years' or less group. Responses in Table 6.3 are percentages.

Table 6.3: Teachers' aims in teaching reading by years of experience

| | | | *Teachers' Experience in Years* | | | | | |
| | P4 | | P5 | | P6 | | P7 | |
Aims	Under 5	Over 5	Under 5	Over 5	Under 5	Over 5	Under 5	Over 5
Enjoyment/Interest	24	26	34	37	52	44	38	40
Comprehension	14	20	16	15	20	21	12	15
Skills	54	35	40	37	20	27	38	29
Information	8	18	10	11	8	8	12	15
Total	100%	99%	100%	100%	100%	100%	100%	99%
Number of Teachers	54	42	45	54	46	59	18	72

A small, but not wholly consistent tendency is for the teachers of less experience to emphasize skills, and the more experienced to emphasize the functional aspects of reading as a means of obtaining information. But there is no sharp distinction between more or less experienced teachers.

An analysis of teachers' reasons for the difference between good and poor readers shows similar absence of clear cut differences. The more experienced teachers tend to attach more weight to pupils' natural ability, but not to any significant extent.

The same lack of any clear distinction between more and less experienced teachers appears in their use of oral reading both by pupil to teacher and by teacher to pupil. But in the use of formal silent reading periods, there is a tendency for teachers with more than five years' experience to use formal silent reading less regularly than do the less experienced teachers ($p=\cdot02$). There is a difference of the same degree of significance ($p=\cdot02$) between the same groups of teachers in respect of their use of homework, where the more experienced teachers tend to dispense with homework to a greater extent than the less experienced teachers. This tendency appears in all classes from P4 to P6. On the other hand, there is no relationship between more and less experienced teachers in their practices of separating or integrating reading and written work.

The suggestion from the evidence is that the younger, or more correctly the less experienced teachers, tend to be a little more exacting in their requirements than the more experienced ones. They tend to emphasize skills in reading a little more, to use silent reading periods and homework to a greater extent than the more experienced teachers. Their reward seems to be marginally better reading progress by their pupils. All in all, however, pupils taught by less or more experienced teachers show little differences in either reading attainment or progress. In any case, the majority of the pupils, during the years under review, have experienced both categories of teachers.

Secondary class teachers

In the secondary schools there is not the same one to one relation between teacher and class. Even within subjects it was not uncommon for subject teachers to share classes, and the use of setting in some schools for some subjects further eroded the simple relationship. As several of the secondary schools were in the process of administrative changes during the period of the investigation, mostly leading to the disappearance of some smaller secondaries in favour of larger comprehensive secondary schools, it did not seem profitable to examine the already very complex school organization when changes were still taking place. The impression gained was that the secondary schools were moving towards a state of uniformity, in which each was becoming more like the others.

Teacher training

Under this heading come pre-service courses for teachers in training at colleges of education, in-service courses conducted by various bodies, mainly colleges of education and education authorities, and services provided by primary advisers, teacher resource centres and the like. The part played by head teachers in guiding probationer teachers has not been included. Teachers are, in fact, subject to advice and guidance from many quarters, but the extent to which this has direct influence on their teaching practices is very difficult to assess. It also depends on the geographical location of the school, the administrative arrangements made and on the felt need by teachers for guidance and assistance in the teaching of reading.

It is therefore not the function of this investigation to make an exhaustive survey of national and local facilities for teacher training, which is a topic in itself, but rather to continue to concentrate on the teachers in the sample under inquiry, and outline as background the facilities available and used. A distinction between primary and secondary teachers is necessary. The primary teachers are all engaged in much the same kind of task, and teaching language, which includes reading, is common to all. In the secondary schools there is division of labour, and active involvement in the teaching of reading is largely confined to English and remedial teachers. The teachers of other subjects require some ability in functional reading in their pupils, are not satisfied with the level of such ability, but do not generally appear to consider it their duty or within their competence to provide instruction or exercises in the reading skills required for the effective study of their subject matter. The provision of guidance and training for secondary teachers in the teaching of reading is therefore very limited indeed, mainly, it appears, because of absence of any articulate demand for it by teachers, and absence of an awareness of a need by the bodies who would provide such training. As there is very little done about training secondary teachers to meet the reading requirements of their teaching and the pupils difficulties in reading arising therefrom, there is relatively little space devoted to the topic in this report. That does not mean it is of no importance. In the secondary school pupils are taught subjects from modern studies to Gaelic, and statistics to Spanish, but they are not taught how to learn or study. The affects of this cannot be assessed in the present investigation; there does, however, seem to be a gap which needs to be filled.

Pre-service training

It is logical to begin at the beginning of the teacher's career, at the college of education, previously training colleges. Ninety-five per cent of the primary teachers in the sample were trained in Scotland, from 1930 to 1974. Their attitudes to preparation they received were roughly four unfavourable to one favourable. The majority of the more experienced teachers preferred not to comment as they regarded their initial training as having become increasingly irrelevant. The main complaint was lack of practicality in the courses, but it must be said on behalf of the colleges that the destination in the schools of the student in training was unknown, so specific preparation for a particular type of teaching duty was not possible. It can also be said that many of the unfavourable comments were contradictory, for example, teacher A: 'too much time spent on younger children'; teacher B: 'not enough time spent on the younger pupils'. But in general teachers are not favourably impressed by their professional training.

During the investigation all the colleges of education and the one university preparing students for a teaching qualification were visited. The institutions training teachers in physical education and domestic sciences were not included, nor were the universities associated with the colleges preparing students for BEd degrees.

Pre-service training (primary)

The basic form of pre-service training, as far as the teaching of reading is concerned, is either a set of coordinated courses given by the primary methods, English and psychology departments, or a more practically biased course conducted mainly by the primary methods department, with some contributions from the English department.

In these schemes reading is dealt with as a part, though a major part, of primary school teaching. The only comment arising from this investigation is that those teachers who complained of too much attention to younger children seem to have some justification. On balance, the courses appeared weighted towards the early stages of learning to read, and towards overcoming reading difficulties. Most courses gave less attention to the upper primary classes and to developing further the skills of the better readers.

Though there were variations from college to college in the basic training system, there are some developments taking place which merit comment. One college at least has in association with a college reading centre, developed a course on the teaching of reading as such, not wholly integrated in more general courses in primary teaching methods. This is still in the early stages, but it should be worthwhile investigating the effects when sufficient teachers move into the primary schools.

Another feature is the development of reading or language centres, associated with both in-service and pre-service courses. These centres act both as resource centres and provide services for courses of study. Again, the organization varies somewhat between centres, and though most have been instituted fairly recently, the use of them by teachers is increasing. The centres tend to be located in fairly populous centres, like Glasgow, Ayr and Falkirk, but even if similar teacher centres run by local authorities are added, there still seems a lack of facilities for teachers in more outlying areas. Perhaps such centres could profitably be set up in each teacher training institution, to make teachers in training familiar with available resources, of all kinds, and at the same time provision be made for extension to more remote areas to enable teachers to continue to use them.

A final feature of some courses of training was the more thorough study by students or groups of students of some topic not common to all students in the course. These assignments, projects, ploys, theses or researches did generate some very thorough investigations and studies by student teachers. It seems possible that these special studies might be developed even more fully, and supplemented by later in-service studies, with a view to creating within the schools a body of teachers whose expertise in the teaching of reading is more than that of most of their colleagues. There are already, rather haphazardly distributed among schools, teachers with more than average interest and competence in areas like drama or games. A number of teachers who could be a source of information and advice on reading would not come amiss, especially if their activities were not confined to problems and difficulties, but included development of the abilities of the more able pupils as well.

Pre-service training (secondary)

With a few exceptions, such as physical education and BEd, secondary teachers are trained during one session. This leaves little time for the reading skills involved in the study of the various subjects. There appears to be Lttle attention devoted to the reading requirements of pupils in the different areas of subject study. The teachers of English are most directly concerned with reading, but here the emphasis appears to be mainly in literary content of reading, and the discussion of technical skills to be orientated to linguistics.

The various centres already mentioned are almost entirely directed to primary teachers; the Centre for Information on the Teaching of English (CITE) is quite properly concerned with reading in English, but there is no evidence that corresponding centres for other secondary subjects make the reading skills assisting effective study a major part of their activities. The reading requirements of secondary schools have been examined in the discussion on functional reading. It can only be added here that this aspect of secondary school teaching plays a very small part in the training of the teachers.

In-service training

There are increasing opportunities for serving primary school teachers to refurbish their attitudes and practices in teaching reading. From the table at the beginning of this chapter, it appears that 23 per cent of the teachers in P4, P5, P6 and P7 have attended courses or seminars which included the teaching of reading. Roughly, attendance over a long weekend or one to two days or a series of evening meetings up to five in number were described as short courses. These courses, both long and short, were normally not wholly devoted to reading, but included reading as one aspect of language studies. Most of the courses involving the remedial teaching of reading were long courses, and compared with the others, more thorough. Currently there is no recognized qualification as a 'remedial' teacher such that all remedial teachers are required to have it.

These in-service facilities are provided by a number of bodies such as colleges of education, usually in association with the reading centres, by education authorities, also in association with teachers' centres, by teachers' associations, mainly as panels investigating a specific aspect of teaching reading, and by universities. It is not profitable to analyse in detail the various channels and agencies of in-service training, which were in any case not used by about 75 per cent of the teachers in the investigation. Apart from the frequency of attendance at courses by the teachers, the other data relevant to in-service training relate to the influence of the primary advisers employed by the education authorities. Teachers were asked how much influence the advisers had on their teaching of reading in the classroom. The responses were virtually the same for all of the primary classes. The response of 'Little or none' was given by 93 per cent of the teachers the remainder replying either 'Some' (six per cent) or 'A lot' (one per cent). It should be made clear that these responses referred only to the direct relationship between primary advisers and class teachers. The influence of the advisers in maintaining teacher centres and organizing courses and seminars was not assessed. But it may be that the 75 per cent of the teachers who had attended no courses could be assisted by more direct communication between advisers and teachers. A final note: the members of this investigating team gained the impression that there was a livelier interest in the teaching of reading in those districts where there had been previous research inquiries into the topic.

About in-service training in the teaching of reading for secondary teachers there is little that can be said. Though the question was not fully investigated, little came to the attention of the investigating team that would suggest that, apart from English and remedial teaching, much if anything was being done about it. The pre-service and in-service positions are much the same.

Conclusion

The training of teachers, even if limited to the teaching of reading, is a major topic in itself. The discussion here has been necessarily confined to current practices, which in pre-service training have very little relevance to the present group of pupils being investigated. In-service training has some relevance, though only affecting about one-quarter of the teachers in the present sample. In the primary schools, the investigation concentrated on the teaching of the upper classes, and in pre-service training there does appear some bias towards the earlier rather than the later stages of primary school reading, and in the preparation for teaching reading to those upper classes, the concentration appears to be more on content of reading material than developing reading skills. Some redress of this imbalance would appear desirable, with a view to preparing pupils for the new and more varied reading demands of the secondary school studies. It does not seem practicable to extend to a significantly large extent the reading aspects of training for all primary teachers, but it does seem that by using the developing facilities of reading or language centres, and developing the special interests of some students in teaching reading, that a number of teachers with special expertise in reading could begin to move into the schools, who could with reinforcement from in-service provisions become in addition to their normal duties a source of information and advice on the teaching of reading.

The various provisions for in-service training appear adequate, except for the administrative difficulties affecting smaller and remoter schools. Possibly some greater emphasis on functional reading skills and requirements would be profitable, as well as provisions for combined courses for upper primary and lower secondary school class teachers.

Training for secondary school teaching of reading, apart from English and remedial teachers, appears to be virtually non-existent. It is not likely that this aspect of training will develop significantly until it is agreed whose duty the teaching of reading is. This is discussed elsewhere in this report.

Appendix

Table 6.1A: Primary class teachers

(a) *Experience*

	Less than 2 years	*2–5 years*	*More than 5 years*	*Total*
P4	24	30	42	96
P5	16	29	54	99
P6	23	22	59	104
—	—	—	—	—
P7	6	12	72	90

(b) *Qualifications*

	Coll. Dip.	*Graduate*	*CD + Infants Cert.*	*Total*
P4	81	12	4	97
P5	81	15	3	99
P6	77	27	1	105
—	—	—	—	—
P7	54	36	0	90

(c) *Experience other than Primary*

	Secondary	*Remedial*	*None*	*Total*
P4	5	3	88	96
P5	3	0	94	97
P6	5	1	97	103
—	—	—	—	—
P7	35	0	56	91

(d) *Training*

	Scotland	*Outwith Scotland*	*Total*
P4	87	6	93
P5	95	3	98
P6	93	4	97
—	—	—	—
P7	81	5	86

(e) *Views on Training*

	Favourable	*Neutral*	*Unfavourable*	*No comment*	*Total*
P4	8	12	37	42	99
P5	17	10	65	7	99
P6	15	7	53	34	109
—	—	—	—	—	—
P7	14	2	39	42	97

(f) *Attendance at Special Courses on Reading*

	None	*Short*	*Long*	*Total*
P4	79	15	2	96
P5	69	16	14	99
P6	84	15	4	103
—	—	—	—	—
P7	64	23	0	87

Chapter 7

Reading in Secondary School

> 'The aristocrat who banks at Coutts,
> The aristocrat who hunts and shoots,
> The aristocrat who cleans our boots,
> They all shall equal be.'
>
> W. S. GILBERT

This chapter deals with the older sample of pupils, those who were first tested by Edinburgh Reading Test in P7, and proceeded through P7 to Sec 1 and Sec 2 and were again tested on the Edinburgh Reading Test at the beginning of Sec 3. During this period from 1972 to 1975, reorganization of secondary education was taking place partly due to changes in local government structure and partly due to the phasing out in some areas of the smaller secondary schools and the development of larger secondary schools of the comprehensive type. The relationship of the primary feeder schools to the area secondary schools changed in some districts during the progress of the inquiry, and the stability of school organization desirable for longitudinal research was not wholly present.

Transfer of P7 to secondary classes

Of the 2515 pupils tested in P7, 2325 or 92·4 per cent appeared in the Sec 1 rolls of the secondary schools. But another 813 pupils, not in the P7 sample, also appeared from various sources in the Sec 1 school rolls, giving the P7 pupils tested a proportion of 74 per cent of all Sec 1 pupils in the fifteen secondary schools selected. The 190 pupils in P7 who did not appear in Sec 1 had an average RQ=97·2, not significantly different from the mean RQ=98·1 of those continuing to secondary school.

By the time the pupils had reached Sec 3, 2757 were tested, but of the original P7 pupils 695 were not tested in Sec 3, and 926 pupils in

Sec 3 had no P7 test record. Here the difference between the two groups was larger. For the 695 'losses', the mean RQ=95·0, and for the 926 'gains' mean RQ=100·2. Interpretation of this difference is not straightforward, as the Sec 3 reading tests were standardized on different populations, so a direct comparison is not proper. There is no doubt that the 'losses' are of lower average attainment than the 'gains', but by how much it is difficult to say. It is very probably less than the 5 points RQ obtained by simple subtraction. Standard deviations of RQ throughout are much the same, $15 \pm$ points RQ, nor are there any significant sex differences.

Secondary school organization

The fifteen secondary schools vary in size from 316 Sec 3 pupils tested to 54 pupils tested, but half lie within the range of 200 to 260 pupils per third year. During the inquiry, the changes in secondary school organization were all towards the establishment of classes of uniform size, with the possible exception of one or two small remedial classes. Of the 105 secondary classes involved, the average size of the 96 non-remedial classes was 33·0 pupils, with virtually no variation within schools and little between schools, the range of 24 to 39 pupils per class being about half that in the primary schools. The mean size of the 9 'remedial' classes was 15·1 pupils. Except for four schools which streamed classes by ability, two grant-aided, one Roman Catholic and one small four-year secondary, and for one large school classifying by ability bands, the eleven classes therein being 4 upper, 5 medium and 2 small poorer classes, the classes within schools were not only virtually the same size but also, in terms of the reading test scores, of virtually the same level of ability.

In the circumstances, where uniformity among classes has been created rather than happened, the comparisons between classes as used in primary schools are pointless. There is also the added difference that pupils attend classes in different subjects, conducted by teachers with different views, practices and experience. Only very broad comparisons can be made in practices more or less common to all teachers and subject areas.

Progress from P7 to Sec 3 classes

As the pupils in P7 were assessed on the Edinburgh Reading Test, Stage 3, standardized on a representative population, and the majority of the pupils in Sec 3 tested on Stage 4 of the Edinburgh Reading Test, standardized on the investigation sample only (representative norms were not available at the time), a direct comparison of reading progress between P7 and Sec 3 was not possible. The average reading quotient for P7 pupils entering secondary school was RQ=98·1 (standard deviation=15·2) and for all pupils tested in Sec 3 was 99·0 (SD=14·8). The difference of RQ=+0·9 tells nothing about progress and probably reflects a difference of standardization procedure.

However, several secondary school teachers considered Stage 4 test too difficult for their poorer Sec 3 readers, and these pupils, selected by the schools, were given the same Stage 3 as was used in P7. The mean RQ in Sec 3 of these 508 pupils was RQ=88·5 (standard deviation=11·8). Of these pupils 393 were tested, on the same test, in both P7 and Sec 3, and with these a direct comparison of progress is possible. In terms of raw test score, the data are in Table 7.1.

Table 7.1: Progress between P7 and Sec 3 (raw score)

P7 Scores	n	Mean Sec 3 Scores			Estimated increase (both)
		Boys	*Girls*	*Both*	
0–19	6	55	49	53	(43)
20–39	72	58	58	58	28
40–59	103	81	83	82	32
60–79	98	111	105	109	39
80–99	52	122	126	123	33
100–119	38	141	134	137	17
120+	24	150+	150+	150+	(22)

Boys ($n = 204$)	Mean score P7 = 63·1	SD = 30·0.
	Mean score Sec 3 = 95·2	SD = 33·3.

Girls ($n = 189$)	Mean score P7 = 70·5	SD = 29·4.
	Mean score Sec 3 = 102·1	SD = 32·5.

Four girls and six boys recorded lower scores in Sec 3 than in P7, and for all 393 the difference between the P7 and Sec 3 raw scores is 31·8 points. This represents quite a substantial improvement, and this inquiry lends no support to the statement that there is a decline in reading ability among the poorer pupils in early secondary school. It would be worth investigating, however, whether this progress is maintained, especially as it is associated with the decline in out of school reading reported in a previous chapter. It is possible that the continued teaching of the kind of reading taught in English and remedial classes is reflected in the reading test scores, but that other styles of reading are not developed adequately, with the possible result that, when the direct teaching of reading ceases, the pupils have not built up adequate independent resources of reading skills to maintain their level of literacy. The critical test would be the assessment of reading attainment after formal teaching of school reading ceased. The absence of the habit of out-of-school reading, rather than any inadequacy in the teaching of reading by English and remedial teachers may be the real source of later illiteracy.

Streamed and mixed ability classes

Of the 105 classes each in Sec 1 and Sec 2, 27 are in the five schools which operate some sort of streaming by ability, four schools by classes, one by broad ability bands. The average RQ in P7 for pupils in these schools was RQ=104·7 and in Sec 3 the corresponding figure was RQ=106·3, a difference of RQ=1·6. The corresponding difference for all schools was RQ=0·9. The greater progress of the streamed schools is neither large nor statistically significant, the conclusion being that there is no evidence that mixed ability classes confer any advantages on the pupils as far as reading attainment is concerned.

Teachers' practices in Sec 1 and Sec 2 classes

Where classes are exposed to some dozen or so different teachers each week, teaching subjects with different requirements, there is likely to be little common element in the pupils' experiences as compared with the single teacher class in a primary school. On the other hand, the organization within secondary schools, with classes of usually equal mixed ability following similar courses, varies relatively little from one secondary school to another, and during the span of this investigation secondary schools were becoming steadily more like each other. In secondary schools the variation was between subjects and teachers within classes, in primary schools the variation was between classes and schools. Only the broadest comparisons between practices can be made, and not all differences involve reading.

The tabulations of teaching practices given below are confined to aspects in which reading is one component, and corresponding P7 practices included for comparison.

Table 7.2: Class organization

	P7	S1	S2
Class teaching only	9	36	63
Any class teaching	48	60	74
Group teaching only	17	11	10
Any group teaching	65	38	19
All Classes	97	84	89

The secondary subject teachers providing the information were throughout those teaching English, history (and modern studies), mathematics, physical and general science, technical subjects, and home economics. Teachers of remedial classes were also included. The trend to greater use of class teaching is clear, and where there is choice, less use of group teaching. Science and home economics practise group teaching most, mathematics and technical least, the latter having a high incidence of individual teaching. These differences are probably determined by the preferences of the teachers and the needs of their subjects. The question was therefore put, whether pupils' reading attainments were a factor in determining class organization. In primary school reading was throughout a factor, but for secondary classes the responses were as in Table 7.3.

Table 7.3: Reading and class organization

Reading involved	S1		S2	
	Yes	No	Yes	No
Non-Remedial classes	47	37	15	74
Remedial classes	11	2	4	2
All	58	39	19	76

The reference to reading attainment clearly diminishes in Sec 2, where no subject shows a majority of teachers taking reading into account. In Sec 1, the subjects giving least weight to reading are technical, home economics and English, the former two presumably because of the practical nature of their subject matter, and English because it is an essential element in the subject for all pupils.

The amount of homework involving reading remains relatively stable across the years. Excluding remedial teachers, who prescribe relatively little or no homework in reading, the data are in Table 7.4.

Table 7.4: Reading homework

	P7	S1	S2
Regular	41	25	34
Occasional	20	25	15
None	32	34	40
All	93	84	89

The teachers of mathematics, technical subjects and, in Sec 2, science make least demands on their pupils reading homework, English and history making most demands.

Table 7.5: Oral reading

Pupil to Teacher	P7	S1	S2
Regular	32	16	7
Occasional	27	37	50
None	8	31	32
Teacher to Pupil			
Regular	20	48	39
Occasional	22	16	21
None	14	20	29

Only in pupil to teacher oral reading is there a clear trend, towards less of it as the classes progress through the schools, and apart from English and remedial classes there is virtually no regular oral reading required of pupils in Sec 1 or Sec 2. The practice of oral reading by the teacher to the pupils is fairly well maintained over the three years, only mathematics and history teachers reducing the amount substantially in Sec 2. Whether the teachers of non-literary subjects continued because of reading deficiencies in their pupils was not recorded, but the practice is fairly widespread.

Table 7.6: Formal silent reading

	P7	S1	S2
Regular	25	43	33
Occasional	7	22	21
None	6	19	35
All	38	84	89

The small number of returns for P7 is mainly due to the number of teachers who reported that they could not readily distinguish formal or prescribed silent reading in the classrooms from the other reading activities. The secondary teachers did not report a similar difficulty. In secondary school there is a trend to less silent reading within classrooms, possibly reflected by a corresponding increase in reading homework (Table 7.4). In Sec 1, all subjects, except technical, use silent classroom reading as a teaching practice, but in Sec 2, mathematics and science show a decreasing incidence of the practice, technical subjects showing a slight increase in classroom reading.

Related to classroom reading is the reading required for projects or assignments.

Table 7.7: Reading for class projects

	P7	S1	S2
A lot	28	27	15
Some	27	21	22
Little or None	2	36	52
All	57	84	89

Again, there was a difference in recording between primary and secondary teachers. Primary teachers not using projects involving reading tended to give 'not applicable' as their reply, whereas secondary teachers tend to give 'none' as their reply. All questions were asked orally in personal interviews, so the difference may reflect a difference in attitudes between the two sets of teachers, in the same way as it was found that primary teachers tended to discuss their pupils, while secondary teachers tended to discuss subject matter and methods. For assignment reading the main practitioners are English, history and home economics in both Sec 1 and Sec 2. There is a clear decrease in such reading requirements in Sec 2 for all subjects except the three mentioned above, which show little change.

Secondary school reading requirements

The most marked, and the most disturbing feature of the comparative analyses of reading requirements in the secondary school is the apparent decrease in reading demands on Sec 2 pupils. Taking the 'little or none' entry alone, for the various aspects of reading activities investigated, and expressing the incidence in percentages, Table 7.8 shows a steady decrease in demand between Sec 1 and Sec 2.

Table 7.8: Frequency (percentages) of no reading requirements in secondary school classes

	S1	S2
No reading involved in class organization	44	83
No reading for projects, etc.	43	58
No formal silent reading in school	23	39
No reading for homework	40	45
No oral reading by pupils	37	36

Apart from oral reading by pupils to teachers, the Sec 2 classes show a consistent increase in the proportion of teachers who require no reading by pupils within or without the school. There is no evidence that the amount of reading required is directly related to the efficiency with which the subjects are taught and learned, but it does appear that Sec 2 pupils are being asked to read less than those in Sec 1. The majority of the pupils were in classes of mixed ability and taking what was substantially a common course. What happens in the following years, when pupils are separated into groups as Certificate and non-Certificate, is not covered by this investigation, but there is the possibility that the less academic pupils may be required to do still less reading, with the risk that they may lose their habits of reading. This, combined with the decline in leisure reading reported in Chapter 5, would seem to justify a further investigation into the teaching of reading for pupils in Sec 3 and Sec 4.

The bulk of the reading demands on pupils are made by the English and history teachers who are mainly responsible for maintaining both the reading requirements during the Sec 1 and Sec 2 years, and probably also for the increase in reading attainment from P7 to Sec 3. The drop in reading demands, therefore, appears most in the other subject areas investigated, home economics excepted.

Granting that the decrease in reading requirements in secondary school classes does not necessarily imply less effective teaching, it remains that for future study either within or beyond the secondary school reading can be expected to play an increasing part, particularly when the support of class teaching is removed. Styles of reading appropriate to different subject studies vary, as had been discussed in Chapter 4. This raises the question as to whose responsibility it is to guide and instruct the pupils in the reading skills appropriate to the subject matter being studied. The absence of any such element in the training courses for most secondary teachers was noted in Chapter 6.

Teacher training

The attitudes of Sec 1 and Sec 2 class teachers to their training is given in Table 7.9.

These attitudes refer to training in general, but when further questioned about the teaching of reading, virtually all teachers, except for English and remedial, reported an absence of any training.

There seem to be three possible lines along which schools can give assistance to pupils in effective methods of study, in which reading skill

Table 7.9: Secondary class 1 and 2 teachers' views of their training

Subject taught	Favourable	Neutral	Unfavourable	All
Maths	0	10	6	16
Technical	0	10	3	13
Home Economics	2	7	4	13
Science	2	10	4	16
History	1	1	16	18
English	2	6	18	26
Remedial	6	7	5	18
All	13	51	56	120

is a major element. It could be the duty of the English teachers to extend the range of their activities in the teaching of reading to meet more directly the needs of other subjects, especially the scientific and technical ones. This would require corresponding extension of training. It could be the duty of the subject teachers to develop and train the pupils in the appropriate reading and study skills. Again, the current teachers are not trained in this aspect of their teaching. It could be the duty of a specialist teacher, of the same order as remedial or guidance teachers, to develop the reading and study skills of all pupils in the appropriate subject areas at the appropriate level. There are currently no such persons. Nevertheless, there appears a need for some steps to be taken, as is confirmed by the degree to which secondary teachers find the reading competence of their pupils unsatisfactory, as reported in Chapter 4. There is neither any obvious solution, nor any established body of teaching skills immediately available, but there is sufficient knowledge about reading skills to make a beginning, and much that requires to be done is concerned with flexibility of reading habits, and with establishing approval of various reading styles by teachers. The teachers of English may encourage their pupils to interpret reading material imaginatively; the next school period the technical teacher may be requiring his pupils to read precisely what is there and nothing more. One style merits no more approval than the other. There is still much to be done in the way of developing methods of guidance to pupils on reading and study, but there is enough to justify some pilot schemes which could be established, monitored and compared.

Books in secondary classes

For the primary school classes it was possible to make a list of the most frequently used readers and textbooks. This is not possible for the secondary classes, as very few titles are mentioned more than once, because classes doing a common course during Sec 1 and Sec 2 generally use the same books. Apart from English, only 'History for Young Scots', 'Modern Mathematics in Schools' (Books 2, 3 and 4) and 'Science for the 70s' receive more than four mentions. In English, novels, poetry and, in Sec 2, drama, are more frequently mentioned than class readers. Class readers, none of which appear frequently in the primary school lists, receive nine mentions each in Sec 1 and Sec 2, but no title is common to more than one school. In Sec 1, 19 titles of novels and poetry are mentioned, and in Sec 2, 21 titles. Only *Kidnapped*, *The Otterburn Incident* and *Tom Sawyer* receive more than one mention. About half the secondary schools have abandoned the use of class readers, and all have some novel reading as part of the English course. All schools give lists of supplementary reading, of a very miscellaneous nature, ranging from 'Biggles' books to 'classics'. The pattern in secondary schools is that of concentration of teaching reading in the English courses, and within these courses a greater emphasis on literary reading material than in primary school, the teaching of literary comprehension continuing with less emphasis and being replaced to a considerable degree by the reading of fiction, poetry and drama. The teaching of functional reading outwith English teaching has virtually disappeared, except for some language exercises.

Chapter 8

Social Class, Intelligence and Sex Differences in Reading

'The rich man in his castle,
The poor man at his gate,
God made them high or lowly
And ordered their estate.'

CHURCH HYMNARY

When asked to give reasons for the difference between good and poor readers, a large number of teachers attributed such differences to home background. The main sociological part of the inquiry appears elsewhere in the discussion on good and poor readers, the contents of which suggest that the importance attached by teachers to social conditions was not misplaced. The information about home background was obtained only for those pupils identified as good or poor readers, in order to identify those sociological factors which revealed the maximum contrasts between pupils' reading attainments, rather than those which may indicate only marginal differences throughout the population and not noticeable by a class teacher. There were two categories of good and poor pupils, those who were good or poor relative to the whole sample population, and those who were good or poor within their classes. Both categories were selected on the same basis, the definition of good readers being those one standard deviation or more of test score above the mean, and poor readers being one standard deviation or more below the mean. In the first category the mean was that of the sample population, in the second that of the school class. There are two possible methods of selecting good and poor groups of readers. One, which has been used earlier the A B C classification by average score of a school class, means determining a proportion of the population which shall contain all good readers or poor readers, for example the top or bottom 25 per cent, regardless of the pupils' actual level of attainment. Basically, it depends on rank order, not reading standard. For class averages it is probably better, but for individual pupils it seemed preferable to establish a given level of attainment, here in terms of reading test score, above which pupils would be called good readers, and correspondingly for poor readers. If the distribution of test scores were symmetrical there would be the same number of good readers as poor but in the P4 classes, who were rather young for the test, there is a greater concentration of pupils among the low scores than the high ones. To establish a standard for good readers, the corresponding standard for poor readers had to be fixed in the lower reaches of test score. In the P4 classes therefore there appear fewer poor than good readers. The poor readers are all poor, but there are some who escape the definition by only a small difference of test score. Though many pupils appear in both categories, they are not necessarily identical, as a good reader in a below average class may be only of average attainment in the whole sample population. Attainment was assessed by reading test score in P4 and P7, unless there was serious discrepancy between test score and teachers' estimate; such pupils were omitted from the good or poor categories. It is the second category, which is discussed here, namely those pupils who are good or poor readers within the same educational circumstances, the same teacher, and the same class.

Social class

There has been developed during the present century a very substantial body of knowledge and expertise in the assessment of pupils' abilities. Whatever the controversy that may surround the use of intelligence tests, at least the properties of such tests are well known. Much the same applies to the assessment of educational attainment, in English and mathematics mainly. There is, however, no corresponding knowledge or techniques in assessment of the social background of pupils. The most widely used scale is the Registrar General's grouping of Social Classes, and this has been used here only for the purpose of comparability with other investigations, and because it is the only commonly accepted scale. The term social class has commonly wider denotation (the traditional coals in the bath, for instance) than the Registrar General's Social Classes justify. The Registrar General's Social Class is not a statement about the social conditions in which a family lives, it is a classification of the occupation of the father, and nothing more. Social class does not refer to housing conditions, to cultural interests, to

mother's education nor to father's education except where the occupation requires certain minimal education standards. Nor are the social
classes closely related to any educational criterion. The grouping of
social classes by the Registrar General is briefly as follows:

Social Class I:	Professional, etc., occupations.
Social Class II:	Intermediate occupations.
Social Class III:	Skilled Occupations:
	(N) non-manual;
	(M) manual.
Social Class IV:	Partly skilled occupations.
Social Class V:	Unskilled occupations.

The following selection of occupations by social class gives some
indication of the kinds of occupations included in different social
classes.

Social Class I:	Accountants, dentists, electronic engineers, librarians, pharmacists, University teachers.
Social Class II:	Aircraft Pilots, actors, authors, artists, athletes, managers, crofters, housemothers and fathers, Ministers of the Crown, opticians, Senior Government officials, School and College teachers.
Social Class III:	(non-manual) Cashiers, draughtsmen, Police Officers, salesmen, secretaries, telegraph operators.
Social Class IV:	Ambulance men, barmen, bricklayers, street hawkers, jewellery workers, telephone operators.

The difficulty of establishing a relation between social class and the
educational, literary or cultural level of the home is most clearly
illustrated by comparison of Class I and Class II. In an educational
context, the differences between university and college teachers, or
between accountants and senior governmental officials, or between air-
craft pilots and electronic engineers appear to be very slight indeed. If
Classes I and II are combined, as is done here, that difficulty is removed
but at the expense of classifying athletes' managers, crofters and house

mothers and fathers with people of a high level of academic and professional education. It must be repeated, therefore, that discussion of
social classes can refer only to the groups of fathers' occupations as
categorized by the Registrar General (*Classification of Occupations:*
Office of Population Censuses and Surveys, HMSO, 1970). The extent to
which this classification of occupations also represents a classification
of the pupils' home backgrounds in educational terms is an open
question.

Social class and reading progress with school classes

The six Registrar General's Social Classes are here combined into
four groups. In the P4 classes the incidence of pupils is as in Table 8.1.

Table 8.1: Good and poor readers by social class (P4)

	Social Class				
	I+II	*III (Non-man.)*	*III (Man.)*	*IV+V*	*All*
No. Good readers	121	38	183	82	424
No. Poor readers	53	16	128	79	276
Grant-aided schools only					
No. Good	29	0	0	0	29
No. Poor	27	0	1	0	28
Ratio Good/Poor (All) corrected to equal frequency	1·5/1	1·5/1	0·9/1	0·7/1	1/1

The concentration of pupils from Social Classes I and II in the
Grant Aided schools is obvious, but this is a reflection on the manner of
selection, and not of the distinction between good and poor readers within school classes. The number of good and poor readers in classes within
Grant Aided schools is virtually the same, and there is no reason to
exclude these classes. The data in Table 8.1 reveal, as expected, a
greater proportion of good readers from the non-manual social classes,
but the amount of exception must be emphasized. Within the school
classes, for example, for every ten pupils from homes of semi-skilled or
unskilled manual workers, who are poor readers, there are seven who
are among the good readers in their school class. Teachers who general-
ize and expect poor reading from pupils from such homes are mistaken.

By the time the P4 pupils reached P7, about 68 per cent of the good
readers and 70 per cent of the poor readers had remained in their school
classes and had taken both the P4 and P7 reading test. At the P7 stage,
the pupils were separated into good and poor readers in the same way as

was done in P4. This gave 432 good readers and 397 poor readers. The social class of the pupils now in P7 was not ascertained, but the original good and poor readers in P4 could be identified. Their progress is as shown in Table 8.2, where Good-Good refers to those pupils who were good readers in both the P4 and P7 classifications, and Good-Other means good in P4, but neither good nor poor in P7.

Table 8.2: Reading progress P4 to P7, by social class

		Social Class			
	I + II	*III (Non-man.)*	*III (Man.)*	*IV + V*	*All*
Good–Good	51	18	81	38	188
Good–Other	36	10	43	12	101
Poor–Poor	21	2	34	33	90
Poor–Other	18	5	50	29	102
Per cent good remaining good	59	64	65	76	65%
Per cent poor remaining poor	54	(29)	40	53	47%

The fact that the original P4 poor readers have not remained in the poor category to the same extent as the good readers have maintained their position within school classes is not surprising, as the differences in P4 test score dividing poor from others are very small. A marginal change of score would change the category. What at first sight may be unexpected is the way in which good readers in Social Class IV and V have maintained their positions relative to those in Social Classes I and II. But the explanation may be much the same. If the grant-aided schools are excluded, the 59 per cent good-good in Social Classes I and II, becomes 71 per cent. In the classes in grant-aided schools the standard of reading attainment within classes is relatively high, and again a small change of score may alter category.

Nevertheless, it remains that the good readers from Social Classes IV and V maintain their position within their school classes as well as, or better than their classmates from other Social Classes.

Social class and reading in P7 and secondary classes

When the good and poor readers were identified within the P4 classes, a similar classification on the same principles was made for the P7 pupils. These pupils progressed into secondary school at the end of the session and were tested again in third year secondary. The distribution for good and poor readers in the P7 classes is given in Table 8.3.

Table 8.3: Good and poor readers by social class (P7)

	I+II	*III (Non-man.)*	*III (Man.)*	*IV+V*	*All*
		Social Class			
No. Good readers	124	37	182	79	422
No. Poor Readers	35	23	152	134	344
Grant-aided schools only					
No. Good	28	1	1	0	30
No. Poor	15	2	1	0	18
Ratio Good/Poor (All) corrected to equal frequency	2·9/1	1·3/1	1/1	0·5/1	1/1

When the P7 data are compared with the corresponding data obtained in the same school session for P4 classes, it appears that the relationship of good and poor readers with social class is closer. It may be that social class differences do develop between P4 and P7, or it may be sampling differences between two sets of classes. In view of the way in which the remaining P4 pupils in the 1975 session P7 classes have maintained their status as good or poor (Table 8.2), the second explanation cannot be ruled out. This aspect of the inquiry leads to no firm conclusion on this point.

The assessment of the progress of those pupils in the first and second year of secondary school is more complicated than the relatively straightforward comparison of classes between P4 and P7. Adjustments to equate scores on the two different stages of the reading test, the different practices in selection of pupils for remedial teaching, and the different policies of streaming or creating classes of equal ability all make the comparison between P7 and Sec 3 classes only approximate. In the end, it appeared best to classify Sec 3 pupils as Good and Poor within schools rather than within classes, and it is on this basis that Table 8.4 is constructed. Four schools have been omitted for technical reasons, mainly redistribution of the feeder primary catchment areas.

With the proviso that the figures in Table 8.4 are approximate, it appears that there is little difference by social class in the reading progress of either good or poor readers in the first two years of secondary school, with one possible exception, the good readers in Social Classes IV and V maintaining their reading status to a lesser degree than the others. The poor readers in P7 show more change of status than the good readers, but this could be as much due to loss of pupils between P7 and Sec 3 as changes in reading standards. The average P7 reading scores of

Social Class, Intelligence and Sex Differences in Reading 93

Table 8.4: Reading progress P7 to Sec 3 by social class

	I+II	Social Class III (Non-man.)	III (Man.)	IV+V	All
P7: No. Good Readers	94	36	160	73	363
Sec 3: No. remaining Good	51	16	76	26	169
Sec 3: Per cent remaining good	54%	44%	48%	36%	47%
P7: No. Poor Readers	19	21	142	126	308
Sec 3: No. remaining Poor	5	7	42	35	89
Sec 3: Per cent remaining Poor	26%	33%	30%	28%	29%

pupils not appearing in Sec 3 classes was, as noted previously, below average. The important finding is that relative progress of poor readers between P7 and Sec 3 is not related to social class. With good readers, progress is maintained in Social Classes I and II to a greater extent than in Social Classes IV and V. This, it may be noted, is also a feature of the primary classes (Table 8.2).

The main point emerging is that, given the initial differences in reading attainment by social class, the progress of pupils within their school classes is not in general closely related to Social Class. One element in the relationship may be the fact that the classification of occupations bears no established relationship to the literacy of the home. The expectation that a higher proportion of good readers will appear in Social Classes I and II and conversely a higher proportion of poor readers in Social Classes IV and V is in general confirmed. Whether this difference can be attributed to the differences of average intelligence between social classes, or to differences in home background, is a question that the evidence from this investigation cannot answer. The differences in attainment by social class are, however, already established in P4, and the expectation that good readers within a school class will deteriorate to a greater extent if they come from homes of unskilled or semi-skilled workers is not justified in the later primary school classes and only to a limited extent in the early secondary school. Progress of poor readers appears to be unrelated to social class difference.

Sex differences in reading attainment

In all primary classes in schools other than the two grant-aided schools, boys and girls at the same stage were taught in the same class.

It is possible, therefore, to make a direct comparison between the reading attainment of boys and girls who received the same teaching and took the same test. The comparisons for average attainment and standard deviation are given in Table 8.5. Except for P4, scores are in reading quotients, and grant-aided schools are not included.

The only significant difference is in P5, where girls reach a higher level of attainment than boys. This may be developmental, the difference disappearing two years later when the pupils reach P7. Apart from this one occasion, the differences between boys and girls are negligibly small and not significant. Standard deviations are on balance greater for boys than girls, but differences are again small. In practice, no teacher would notice any consistent superiority of boys over girls, or vice versa. Nor is there a difference in range of attainments between boys and girls which would consistently attract the teachers' attention. Sex equality seems to prevail.

Table 8.5: Edinburgh reading test means and standard deviations by sex

Year	ERT Stage	Class	Boys	Girls
1972	2	P4		
	Mean RS		25·1	25·2
	SD RS		17·0	18·9
1973	2	P5		
	Mean RQ		97·2	99·7
	SD RQ		15·3	15·3
1975	3	P7		
	Mean RQ		97·5	96·7
	SD RQ		15·1	14·5
1972	3	P7		
	Mean RQ		96·6	96·4
	SD RQ		14·4	14·4
1975	3 + 4	Sec 3		
	Mean RQ		97·0	97·4
	SD RQ		14·2	12·9

Intelligence and reading attainment

In 1972, P7 classes in the sample either sat a group Verbal Reasoning Test (Moray House 74) or had scores from this test on record. The one exception to this was Glasgow, where the pupils had taken a different set of verbal group intelligence tests. As these tests had been standardized for Glasgow schools only, and not nationally, the schools in Glasgow have been omitted from any data on IQs, or more correctly VRQs. It should also be made clear that these schools were not selected to represent all Glasgow schools; they were selected to represent schools in Council housing estates and in older city centre areas. The average reading quotient for P7 classes (Glasgow excluded) was RQ=99.4 and the average Verbal Reasoning Quotient was VRQ=98·3. Standard deviation for RQ=15·4, and for VRQ=13·2. As the two tests were standardized in the same way, the close correspondence of average level of performance is not unexpected. The smaller standard deviation for VRQ is not of any educational importance.

More important is the degree of correspondence between pupils' scores on the two tests. This is expressed as a correlation coefficient, r. This is an index figure, not strictly a quantity, such that perfect correspondence is expressed as $r=+1·0$, no correspondence as $r=0$, and perfect inverse correspondence as $r=-1·0$. The correspondence found here was $r=+0·83$, which is high for an educational investigation. Within classes the values of r ranged from $+0·6$ to $+0·9$, with the higher values predominating.

The interpretation of this relationship is far from simple. On the face of it, the close correspondence between the Verbal Reasoning Test scores and the Reading Test scores would indicate that what has been called here natural ability is far and away the major factor contributing to reading attainment. But the only available measure of natural ability is a verbal test, involving reading competence and containing elements, such as vocabulary, common to both tests. The Verbal Reasoning Test and the Edinburgh Reading Test, Stage 3, can almost be regarded as different versions of the same test. This does not invalidate either test, not only because language is the principal vehicle of thought, but also because those factors which influence the development of intelligence could equally influence the development of reading ability. To attempt to distinguish between the influence on reading attainment of natural ability on the one hand, and social and educational conditions on the other, is to enter a longstanding controversy which this investigation was not intended to solve. It is sufficient to say here that the more detailed discussion and analyses of socioeconomic factors do not imply that these necessarily play a larger part in the reading attainments of pupils. There is no doubt but that differences of intelligence, or natural ability, do distinguish between the attainments of pupils with similar educational histories. What cannot be identified here is the proportion in which pupils' abilities and pupils' social circumstances each influence reading attainment and progress.

Differences between VRQ and RQ

The correspondence between VRQ and RQ is close, but not perfect. It was possible to identify these classes whose average reading quotient was substantially greater or less than their average Verbal Reasoning Quotient. Twelve P7 classes had mean VRQs four or more points higher than their mean RQs, the differences ranging from 4·1 to 10·0. A corresponding twelve classes with higher average RQs than VRQs, the difference here ranging from 4·6 to 12·6 points. The mean VRQs and RQs of pupils in the VRQ plus classes (i.e. those with higher mean VRQ than RQ) were VRQ=98·2 and RQ=92·7, a difference of 5·5 points. The corresponding values for the RQ plus classes were VRQ=100·5 and RQ 107·5, a difference of 7·0 points. The difference between the groups was mainly one of reading quotient, the difference in mean VRQ between the groups being 2·3 points whereas the difference in mean RQ was 14·8 points. With the exception of the classes from the grant-aided schools, who appeared only in the RQ plus group, and the classes from smaller schools who featured more frequently in the VRQ plus group, the classes came from very similar kinds of schools, Roman Catholic, urban and small burgh schools appearing in both lists. Glasgow schools were excluded as VRQs were not comparable with the others, most schools did not appear in either list, and not all classes from the schools which did appear in the list showed sufficient difference between mean VRQ and RQ to qualify for inclusion.

The two sets of twelve classes were compared in respect of the variables investigated in this inquiry, and those in which the most marked differences appeared are given in Table 8.6.

For other variables there was even less distinction between the groups. For example, all twelve VRQ plus classes had teachers of more than five years' experience, and eleven of the RQ plus group had such teachers; fifty per cent of each group had regular reading homework, and the incidence of oral reading by pupils was almost the same for both groups.

Of the variables listed, none shows a significant statistical difference between the two groups, but cumulatively a broad picture of differences can be discerned. Classes with average reading quotients higher than verbal reasoning quotients tend to be larger, homogeneous,

Table 8.6: Difference of mean RQ and VRQ by class variables

Variable	VRQ Plus	RQ Plus
(a) No. pupils per teacher	29·0	31·0
(b) No. composite classes	5	0
(c) Class organization		
Class only	5	2
Group only	5	6
Class + Group	0	3
(d) Teacher's aims for reading		
Interest enjoyment	9	4
Comprehension	2	3
Others	6	6
(e) Home encouragement		
All class	3	7
50%	6	4
Few or none	3	1
(f) Reading and writing		
Integrated	4	8
Mixed	4	0
Separate	2	2

have teachers placing less emphasis on Interest and Enjoyment in reading, have more home encouragement and tend to have more frequently integrated reading and writing. But it must be emphasized that these differences are not firmly established by the evidence, and may well be chance differences, especially where they are not in agreement with the other findings of this investigation based on a larger number of classes. Comparisons based on 24 classes from a possible 97 classes are not too reliable.

The conclusion remains that the correspondence between attainment on Verbal Reasoning Tests and Reading Tests is so close that it is not profitable to try to separate them. Relationship with social factors is much the same for the two tests, and to what extent reading attainment and progress are influenced by these factors and intellectual ability separately, it is not possible to say. Teaching probably helps to develop competence both in verbal reasoning and reading. What this investigation shows is that the observed differences in teaching practices are themselves of little significance.

Chapter 9

Good and Poor Reading in Primary School:

Socioeconomic and Related Factors

Graham F. Atherton

There are certain advantages to be had from a separate study of high and low achievers in the school population, as distinct from an *in toto* analysis of pupils drawn from the whole achievement range. Issues affecting good or poor readers are not likely to be clouded over by a concentration upon pupils of 'average' attainment. It is known, for example, that social environment affects the performance of the more able pupil to a greater extent than the less able (Frazer, 1959). In addition, by holding constant initial attainment, it is possible to assess any cumulative changes, which may in turn be related to differences in social environment or educational treatment. Teachers might also be expected to attach greater significance to statements concerning 'bright' and 'backward' pupils than to a discussion of marginal differences in test scores of pupils generally. Finally, there is the consideration that in a wide-ranging survey of this sort, it is not always possible to collect useful background information about all pupils in the sample, and when this is the case, it is perhaps best to concentrate on pupils falling at either end of the achievement range. This chapter is focused on some of the factors related to the subsequent progress of children identified as good or poor readers in their fourth year of primary school. The children were tested in autumn 1972, with Stage 2 version of the Edinburgh Reading Test, and Stage 3 of the test was then administered three years later, when children had reached their seventh and final year of primary school at the age of 11 plus. A parallel investigation was conducted among pupils attending primary 7 classes in 1972 and who were again tested in their third year of secondary school in autumn 1975, but for the sake of clarity in presentation this second group of pupils is considered separately in another chapter. Henceforth, discussion will be confined to pupils moving from primary 4 to primary 7.

Some 2527 pupils in primary 4 completed Stage 2 in 1972 and 2411 pupils completed the Stage 3 version administered to primary 7 classes in the same schools three years later. Pupils were then classified into good or poor readers, for each test sample separately, if their scores exceeded the sample mean by either plus or minus one standard deviation respectively. This is a generally accepted procedure for identifying high and low achievers and has been adopted in other investigations (Wilson, 1972: ILEA, 1975). Pupils with test scores outside the standard deviation range could be expected to represent about a third of the total numbers tested, assuming a normal distribution of scores, with an even balance of high and low achievers. This was, in fact, the case in the present test sample, but there was an uneven representation of good readers (18 per cent of the test sample) compared with poor readers (15 per cent of the sample). Between test sessions, there were gains and losses of pupils as a result of turnover and absence of pupils in school. Of the pupils completing the test in primary 4, 71·5 per cent were retested in primary 7. But there was evidence that pupils lost from the sample and those added to the sample as children moved up the school were of similar average attainment as the 'core' group. The two test samples could therefore be regarded as drawing upon very similar achievement populations. It was then possible to determine whether pupils identified as good or poor readers in primary 4 maintained the same relative positions in the primary 7 test sample. Good readers were deemed to have deteriorated or regressed in performance if they were not re-classified as good readers in primary 7. Poor readers were said to have improved if they were no longer identified as poor in primary 7. In fact, 34 per cent of the good readers had fallen back and 42 per cent of the poor readers had improved. To some extent, these figures are an artefact of the classification procedure adopted; they also reflect relative, not absolute, changes in performance over time.

Statistical regression effects due to test unreliability may also account for some of the observed changes in progress, but a precise estimate for different tests at three years' interval is not possible. The factors investigated in the inquiry included the socioeconomic status of the school neighbourhood, the fathers' occupations of pupils, teachers' estimates of levels of home encouragement, the type of school attended, the amount of reading done out of school hours, and selected practices and attitudes of class teachers. Some of them could have bearing on the chances that good or poor readers were likely or not likely to remain so by the end of primary school.

School neighbourhood

Before the progress of good and poor readers was examined in any detail, however, an assessment was made of the overall contribution of socioeconomic environment to school reading performance. Table 9.1 (p. 111) shows the correlation between school attainment and 1971 Census indices related to the school catchment area.[1] In several instances there are high correlations between school performance and items selected from the census tabulations. Schools were likely to perform well in areas with a high proportion of non-manual household heads, this item being the best predictor of school achievement. Schools were also likely to achieve higher standards in reading where there was a higher incidence of owner-occupier housing or where there were many employed persons with good educational qualifications (highers plus or equivalent). Schools were likely to do least well in areas with a lot of overcrowding (1·5 persons or more per room) or with many large families (containing four or more dependent children). Achievement was further likely to be depressed in neighbourhoods with many one-parent families or children in the 5-14 age range, although these factors appeared to be less important than overcrowding and the family size. Of relatively minor significance was the incidence of female employment or the number of households with exclusive use of standard amenities (bath, hot water, w.c.) perhaps on account of the narrower range of differences between areas on these two items.

The combined effects of the census indices are summarized by the squared multiple correlation coefficients (corrected for sample size and number of predictors) at the foot of Table 9.1. At the primary 4 level, neighbourhood factors 'explained' 44 per cent of differences in achievement between schools. School neighbourhood assumed even more importance as pupils moved into primary 7, where census indices accounted for 68 per cent of school differences in reading standards. School neighbourhood was also more strongly related to the achievement of girls than boys, particularly at the earlier age level, where census indices accounted for 37 per cent of between-school differences for boys and 64 per cent of between-school differences for girls. Furthermore, there is evidence that neighbourhood status is more highly associated with the incidence of good than poor reading in school. In other words, poor readers were more evenly distributed over different types of neighbourhoods than were good readers, perhaps, as Wiseman (1964) has suggested, because schools are more concerned with raising reading standards to an acceptable minimum than with promoting individual excellence above the norm. The residual effects of social environment would accordingly be more manifest among pupils of above average attainment, with very able pupils living in poor neighbourhoods not reading as well as they might.

On account of their high intercorrelations, census indices were subsequently merged into a composite measure of school socioeconomic status. Schools of 'high' socioeconomic status, located in administrative centres and commuter belts, accounted for 45 per cent of the good readers and 18 per cent of the poor readers in the primary 4 sample. Schools of 'medium' status, found mainly in small self-contained industrial communities, accounted for slightly more poor readers than good readers. Over half of the poor readers and a third of the good readers attended schools of 'low' socioeconomic status, serving children living in large council estates and inner-city zones.

When the progress of the good and poor readers was followed up, schools of high socioeconomic status achieved only slightly better results than schools of lower rank (Table 9.2.2). Deterioration in performance occurred among 28 per cent of the good readers in schools of high socioeconomic status but among 35 per cent of good readers in other schools, a difference which failed to reach statistical significance. Among the poor readers, attendance at schools of low socioeconomic status was less likely to result in improvement than in schools of higher status.

Social class[2]

As anticipated, children whose parents were employed in non-manual occupations (Registrar General's classification) were over-represented among the good readers and under-represented among the poor readers. Over 33 per cent of the good readers and only 11 per cent of the poor readers in primary 4 came from non-manual origins; pupils of skilled manual origin accounted for 43 per cent of the good readers and 47 per cent of the poor readers; while 23 per cent of the good readers and 41 per cent of the poor readers were from semi- and unskilled social background. Differences were more marked among girls than boys. The follow-up of good and poor readers into primary 7 indicated that social class was cumulative in its effect. As Table 9.2.3 shows, good or poor readers from non-manual backgrounds made better progress than those from manual backgrounds. Some 20 per cent of non-manual readers had fallen behind, compared with 36 per cent of skilled manual and 45 per cent of semi- and unskilled manual good readers. Social class differences were less marked among the poor readers, but children of non-manual origin were still more likely to improve in their reading than those of manual origin.

Combined effects of school neighbourhood and social class

When the social class background of pupils, as measured by father's occupation, was held constant, schools of high socioeconomic status still contained a 'surplus' of good readers and a 'deficit' of poor readers. They accounted for 60 per cent of the good readers but only 24 per cent of the poor readers coming from non-manual backgrounds. They also represented 39 per cent of the good readers and only 16 per cent of the poor readers from manual backgrounds. In other words, pupils attending schools in the most favoured neighbourhoods were much more likely to be good than poor readers, regardless of whether they were of non-manual or manual origin. Conversely, pupils attending schools of low socioeconomic status, in the most 'deprived' neighbourhoods, were more likely to be poor readers than good readers, even where they were of similar social class origin. Only eight per cent of non-manual good readers but 35 per cent of non-manual poor readers were found in schools of low socioeconomic status. Educational selection operates within as well as between social classes, ensuring that the more able elements from each social class are concentrated in schools serving the best neighbourhoods.

There was only partial support for the view that the superior performance of pupils attending schools of high socioeconomic status was the *result* of superior schooling. When the progress of good and poor readers was analysed by type of school attended, holding social class constant, pupils of non-manual origin seemed to benefit substantially from attending a school in a good neighbourhood (Table 9.2.4.), whereas pupils of manual origin did not (Table 9.2.5). Only 12 per cent of non-manual good readers regressed if they attended a school of high socioeconomic status, but 42 per cent of them fell behind in schools of lower rank. Similarly, among poor readers from non-manual backgrounds, nine out of 10 pupils in schools of high status had improved but only six out of 13 pupils in other schools had done as well, a difference which achieved statistical significance, despite the small numbers involved. But school socioeconomic status had no bearing on the progress of pupils from manual backgrounds. Good or poor readers from manual backgrounds who attended schools in the best neighbourhoods made no more progress than either non-manual or manual pupils attending schools in the least favoured areas. For non-manual pupils,

reading progress seems to be enhanced where there is integration between the learning environment of the home and that of the school,
a factor which is not so critical for manual pupils.

Home encouragement as rated by Primary 4 Teachers[3]

Teachers estimated that six per cent of the good readers and 41 per
cent of the poor readers in primary 4 came from homes where encouragement to read was poor or unsatisfactory. Teachers' assessments
were also related to the social class backgrounds of pupils. Homes were
judged unsatisfactory for none of the good readers from non-manual
backgrounds, but for nine per cent of the good readers from manual
backgrounds. Poor home encouragement was also reported for 19 per
cent of poor readers from non-manual backgrounds but for 36 per cent
of poor readers from skilled manual backgrounds and for 49 per cent
of poor readers from semi- and unskilled origins. Assessments made by
teachers in primary 4 were important predictors of progress achieved by
pupils three years later. The number of good readers coming from poor
home backgrounds was too small for statistical analysis; but improvement occurred among 52 per cent of the poor readers in homes where
encouragement had been rated good or satisfactory, whereas only 27
per cent of poor readers from unsatisfactory homes did as well (Table
9.2.6). When social class background, as measured by fathers' occupation, was held constant, poor readers from satisfactory homes continued
to show a higher rate of improvement than poor readers from unsatisfactory homes. Teachers' assessments were unrelated to school socioeconomic status, however.

School attendance as rated by primary 4 class teachers[3]

Only two per cent of good readers and 12 per cent of poor readers had
unsatisfactory attendance records, according to primary 4 teachers'
estimates. To monitor weekly attendance returns appeared to be
unnecessarily laborious, and teachers' estimates, subjective though
they may sometimes be, were preferred as it was more likely that
teachers distinguished between necessary and unnecessary absence.
Nor is there a numerical definition of unsatisfactory.

Grant-aided schools

Over 22 per cent of the good readers and under one per cent of the
poor readers were attending the two grant-aided schools in the sample.
Almost all of them came from professional and managerial social class

backgrounds. Attendance at a grant-aided school resulted in a much better progress record among the good readers between primary 4 and primary 7, compared with performance in education authority schools (Table 9.2.8). There was also some evidence that grant-aided pupils fared slightly better than pupils of non-manual background attending public schools, as comparison between the top entries of Tables 9.2.3 and 9.2.8 reveals. This may be the result of more positive parental attitudes among the grant-aided pupils as well as a product of better schooling.

Denominational schools[4]

Pupils attending denominational (Roman Catholic schools) fared no differently from pupils in other schools. There was an even representation of good and poor readers in both types of school, despite the preponderance of pupils from manual backgrounds attending denominational schools. The progress of the good readers was not significantly affected by type of school, but poor readers were somewhat less likely to improve if they attended a denominational school (Table 9.2.8). The latter finding was mainly the result of many poor readers coming from a semi- and unskilled home background, rather than the outcome of denominational schooling.

Out of school reading

Unlike socioeconomic background, there has been a paucity of research on pupils' out-of-school reading activities: the only recent study being that of Whitehead *et al.* (1974). Results from the current investigation clearly indicate that the amount of reading done out of school in a sample week is an important index of the amount of reading progress likely to be achieved in the years ahead (Table 9.3.1). But the relationship between the amount of reading done out of school and reading attainment is by no means straightforward. Although the majority of good readers reported reading books after school, some 17 per cent of good readers claimed to have read no books at all during the week sampled, while 22 per cent of poor readers said they had read at least two books in their own time. (These figures relate to pupils in primary 4 classes). Good readers who mentioned the titles of two or more books in primary 4 made greater progress over the following three years than those who mentioned fewer books. Poor readers who mentioned two or more books were similarly advantaged, 64 per cent of them showing improvement compared with only 35 per cent of poor readers mentioning fewer books. The pattern was repeated to a lesser extent when pupils were asked to mention the names of any magazines, newspapers or comics they had read in their leisure time (Table 9.3.2). Better progress was achieved even among pupils (mainly poor readers) whose out-of-school reading consisted only of comics, compared with pupils who read nothing at all. None of the difference in out-of-school reading habits was related to social class; there was as much reading reported among good or poor readers of manual background as of non-manual background. The correlation between out of school reading and social class, which has been observed by other investigators, disappears when reading test performance is held constant.

Practices and attitudes of class teachers

Information of the practices and attitudes of class teachers was collected over three successive sessions, in primary 4, 5 and 6 classes, and related to the progress of the good and poor readers between test sessions. Data on the incidence of various classroom practices and teachers' attitudes are presented more fully elsewhere in this report.

1. Reading laboratories

Slightly more good than poor readers were found in primary 4 classes where teachers made use of reading laboratories. Good and poor readers also fared better in classes where reading labs had been in use during three successive sessions than where use was more restricted but differences were not statistically significant (Table 9.4.1).

2. Use of textbooks for activities other than English and maths

Half of the good readers and only a third of the poor readers came from primary 4 classes where no use was made of standard textbooks for activities other than basic subjects, 'projects' being the major form of study where resort to textbooks was limited. Poor readers were more likely than good readers to be found in classes where textbooks were used in social and science studies except for grant-aided schools. Table 9.4.2 indicates that the progress of the good readers was unaffected by the use of textbooks between test sessions, but improvement among the poor readers was more likely to occur when textbooks were used only for English and maths. It would appear that teachers resort to textbooks where reading standards are generally low. Textbooks were in greater use among Roman Catholic schools compared with other types of school, with the exception of grant-aided schools, where textbooks were also used a lot.

3. Homework provisions

Some 32 per cent of the good readers and 17 per cent of the poor readers were represented in primary 4 classes where no homework was issued at all, over two or more sessions. Poor readers were more likely to be found in classes where homework involving regular prescribed reading was the norm. But there was no evidence that homework provisions were responsible for the subsequent progress of good and poor readers. Only good readers attending classes where no homework was given between test sessions were at a slight disadvantage, a finding which failed to achieve statistical significance (Table 9.4.3). Homework provisions seem to be a result rather than a cause of differences in reading attainment, with greater emphasis being placed on homework where reading standards are low.

4. Comics in class

Teachers were divided in their views about permitting pupils to read comics in the classroom. Slightly more good than poor readers came from classes where reading comics was discouraged. Table 9.4.4 shows that the progress of the good readers was unaffected by teachers' attitudes to comics, while poor readers were more likely to improve in classes where comics were permitted than where they were discouraged.

5. Book supply

Similar proportions of good and poor readers in primary 4 were represented in classes where teachers expressed satisfaction or dissatisfaction with the availability of books in school. Teacher satisfaction or dissatisfaction was unrelated to the progress of the good readers, but a lower incidence of improvement occurred among poor readers whose class teachers offered contrary views from one session to the next (Table 9.4.5).

6. Nature of reading

Teachers' open-ended responses could be divided into those defining reading in (a) purely instrumental terms, (b) as a basic comprehension skill required for effective functioning in school, (c) as a source of enjoyment and information, and (d) multiple responses (both within and between sessions). Good and poor readers were fairly evenly represented in classes of primary 4 teachers with different points of view. There was less of a decline in performance among good readers in classes where teachers stressed enjoyment and information (Table 9.4.6). Progress of the poor readers was not critically affected.

7. *Reasons for differences in reading attainment*

Just under a quarter of the good readers and a third of the poor readers were found in classes where teachers attributed differences in reading attainment to home background factors. A slightly smaller proportion of good than poor readers came from classes where teachers attributed reading attainment to basic ability. The majority of teachers gave multiple explanations and similar proportions of good and poor readers originated from their classes. There was considerably more deterioration among good readers in classes where teachers emphasized home background, but the progress of the poor readers was unrelated to teachers' views (Table 9.4.7).

8. *Average reading attainment of class in primary 4*

The progress of the good and poor readers was not affected by the average reading standard of the class in primary 4. Good readers in classes whose performance was in the lower quartile range were likely to fare only slightly worse than in classes of higher average attainment. Poor readers did not benefit significantly from attendance in classes of above average attainment (Table 9.5.1).

9. *Pupil turnover in class between primary 4 and primary 7*

The progress of good readers was not substantially impaired as a result of attendance in classes where more than 50 per cent of pupils were lost or gained between test sessions, but it did appear that a high turnover rate put the poor readers at some disadvantage (Table 9.5.2). Since several classes were not reconstituted between test sessions, however, it was not possible to make a straightforward assessment.

10. *Length of teaching experience*

Classes taught over two or more sessions by inexperienced teachers (with under two years' service) counted for 11 per cent of the good readers and 21 per cent of the poor readers. Over 24 per cent of the good readers and 10 per cent of the poor readers were taught by teachers with more than five years' experience. None of these differences was statistically significant. There was some indication that the progress of the good readers was impaired where pupils were taught mainly by inexperienced teachers between test sessions, but the progress of poor readers was unaffected by teaching experience (Table 9.5.3). Schools of high socioeconomic status accounted for a significantly higher proportion of teachers with over five years' experience compared with schools of low status, but similar proportions of inexperienced teachers were found in both types of school.

11. Class composition

Slightly more good than poor readers were found in 'composite' classes containing pupils from mixed age groups. Attendance in a composite class did not adversely affect the progress of either good or poor readers (Table 9.5.4), although there is evidence (reported on elsewhere) that pupils of average attainment attending composite classes tend to make poorer progress than pupils in homogeneous age groups.

12. Other factors

A number of other factors were investigated: whether pupils were taught in streamed or unstreamed classes, whether they were taught as a whole class or in groups, whether teachers regarded reading and writing as 'separate' or 'integrated' activities, whether time was set aside in class for silent reading, whether or not teachers emphasized oral methods of teaching, the level of teacher turnover in classes within a single session, whether teachers were graduates or non-graduates, and whether open plan methods or team teaching were practised. These topics are discussed elsewhere. There was insufficient variation between schools, classes or teachers on such items to make a statistical assessment of their association with the progress of good and poor readers.

Summary and conclusions

Socioeconomic background and out of school reading figured as the most important correlates of reading attainment and subsequent progress of the good and poor readers, carrying much more weight than selected practices and attitudes of class teachers. Census indices of school socioeconomic status accounted for a great deal of the variation in reading standards between schools, and superior performance was particularly associated with the presence of many non-manual household heads living in the school neighbourhood. But schools in the most favoured areas not only contained most of the good readers from non-manual backgrounds, they also attracted the greater share of good readers of manual origin. The tendency for school neighbourhood status to discriminate on an intellectual level within as well as between social classes may be the outcome of social and economic policies which force certain types of family, of a certain intellectual disposition and social orientation, to settle in some areas and not in others. Indeed, Robson (1969) observed that working class respondents living in 'well integrated' middle class neighbourhoods entertained educational expectations that were higher than average, and it may be that achievement potential of pupils has been determined before children even enter school There is limited evidence that differences in reading achievement are the direct result of school socioeconomic milieu, but it seems that socioeconomic differences between schools are more important for non-manual than manual pupils. Non-manual pupils, whether good or poor readers, made better progress if they attended a good neighbourhood school than one elsewhere, whereas manual pupils attending schools in the most 'privileged' neighbourhoods fared no better than their counterparts living in more 'deprived' areas. " 'Balancing' the social intake of pupils in school, achieving a greater 'social mix' among pupils is more likely to affect the performance of non-manual than manual pupils, a conclusion supported by Barnes and Lucas (1975) in their comparison of EPA and non-EPA schools."

Of more practical import is the strong relationship between the progress of the good and poor readers and the amount of reading done out of school. The fact that reading pursuits within each of the good and poor groups were unrelated to social background should be a source of encouragement to teachers, who are not entirely at the mercy of external circumstances. None of the classroom factors explored provided a satisfactory explanation of differences in out-of-school reading habits however. Indeed, classroom practices and teachers attitudes were relatively ineffective in accounting for difference in reading achievement generally. Where significant relationships were observed, as with the use or non-use of textbooks outside basic subjects of whether comics were permitted in class, the progress of the poor readers rather than good readers was affected, and it was not possible to establish any casual connections. Other surveys have also found that school or classroom conditions are of limited influence, but it may be that in-depth studies involving classroom observations are now required.

References

BARNES, J. H. and LUCAS, H. (1975) 'Positive discriminations in education: individuals, groups and institutions'. In: *Educational Priority*, Vol. 3: *Curriculum Innovation in London's EPAs*. London: HMSO.

DAVIE, R. *et al.* (1972) *From Birth to Seven:* a report of the National Child Development Study, statistical volume. London: Longmans.

FRAZER, E. (1959) *Home Environment and the School*. London: University of London Press.

ILEA (Inner London Education Authority (1975) *Preliminary Reading Survey*. Available from GLC Bookshop, County Hall, London.

OFFICE OF POPULATION CENSUSES AND SURVEYS (1970) *Classification of Occupations 1970*. London: HMSO.

ROBSON, B. T. (1969) *The Social Ecology of Sunderland*. Cambridge: Cambridge University Press.

WHITEHEAD, F. *et al.* (1974) *Children's Reading Interests*. Schools Council Working Paper No. 52. London: Evans/Methuen.

WILSON, J. A. (1972) *Environment and Primary Education in Northern Ireland*. Belfast: Northern Ireland Council for Educational Research.

WISEMAN, S. (1964) *Education and Environment*. Manchester: Manchester University Press.

Notes

1. School socioeconomic status was assessed by matching and aggregating unpublished Small Area Statistics (Ward Library) of the 1971 Census corresponding to the catchment areas of 42 of the 58 primary schools in the sample. (The catchment areas of two grant-aided schools and eight Roman Catholic schools could not be identified with any precision on account of the wide residential dispersal of pupils attending these schools, while areas served by certain rural schools were combined into larger units to achieve goodness of fit with census tract boundaries.) Items dealing with housing, education, economic activities, and family circumstances were selected from the tabulations and raw frequencies were converted into percentages, which, averaged out over all school areas, corresponded closely to comparable data for the whole of Scotland. There was, however, considerable diversity between school areas in socioeconomic makeup, with, for example, the percentage of non-manual household heads living in the area ranging from 15 to 45 per cent, and the incidence of large families from nil to 25 per cent. Since the census indices were highly intercorrelated, a composite measure of school socioeconomic status was derived from a principal components varimax solution. The weights of indices on the first principal component, which accounted for 55 per cent of the total variance, were used to compute a factor score for each school area. Schools were then rank ordered by their score and assigned to three broad socioeconomic categories, labelled high, medium and low, containing 14 schools each.

2. Schools supplied details of the fathers' occupations of pupils identified as good or poor readers in primary 4. Occupations were coded into non-manual, skilled manual, and semi- and unskilled categories in accordance with procedures described in the Registrar General's Classification of Occupations (Office of Population Censuses and Surveys, 1970). Data on fathers' occupation was unobtainable for 11 per cent of good and poor readers, but comparison with the Scottish seven-year-old cohort of the National Child Development Study (Table A165, in Davie *et al.*, 1972) indicated that pupils came from representative social backgrounds, as below:

	Non-manual	Skilled manual	Semi-skilled	n cases
Scottish Reading Survey:	25·2	45·3	29·5	(572)
NCDS Scottish cohort:	22·9	47·8	29·3	(1599)
		(row percentages)		

3. Teachers' assessments relate to individual pupils classified as good or poor readers.

4. Results were based on a questionnaire completed by pupils in the summer terms of 1973 and 1975. Pupils were asked to state the titles of any books, comics, newspapers, or periodicals they had read out of school over the previous seven days.

Table 9.1: Correlations between mean reading attainments of pupils grouped by school and 1971 census indices of school socioeconomic status (n=42 primary schools)

	Primary 4			Primary 7		
1971 Census indices	*Boys*	*Girls*	*All*	*Boys*	*Girls*	*All*
percentages	*only*	*only*	*pupils*	*only*	*only*	*pupils*
Non-manual hh heads	·40	·66	·63	·68	·74	·70
Owner-occupied housing	·17	·55	·36	·60	·58	·55
Employed with Highers +	·34	·60	·56	·63	·59	·54
Families with 4+ children	−·40	−·73	−·54	−·68	−·60	−·63
Hh with 1·5+ persons per room	−·24	−·55	−·37	−·61	−·45	−·49
Single-parent families	−·10	−·25	−·19	−·11	−·45	−·39
Families with children aged 5–14	−·15	−·35	−·28	−·29	−·40	−·33
Married women in employment	−·10	−·03	−·08	−·05	−·15	−·10
Hh with exclusive amenities	·18	·04	·12	·08	·01	·05
Per cent variance explained by census indices combines (R^2c)	·37	·64	·44	·64	·71	·68

Table 9.2: Progress of good and poor readers between primary 4 and primary 7: socio-cultural factors

	P4 Good Readers		P4 Poor Readers	
		Per cent		*Per cent*
	N	*who*	*N*	*who*
Total sample†	*pupils*	*deteriorate*	*pupils*	*improve*
	228	32·0	223	41·7
1. Sex: Boys	111	35·9	105	45·7
Girls	117	27·9	118	38·1
2. School socioeconomic status: High	92	28·3	39	48·7 ⎫ *
Medium	32	32·4	47	48·1 ⎭
Low	67	37·0	76	34·5*
3. Social class: Non-manual	75	20·0**	28	65·2*
Skilled manual	96	36·5**	94	43·6*
Semi-skilled manual	51	45·1**	82	40·2*
4. Non-manual pupils:				
School socioeconomic status: High	40	12·5*	10	90·0*
Medium	14	21·4*	8	50·0 ⎫ *
Low	12	41·7*	5	40·0 ⎭
5. Manual pupils:				
School socioeconomic status: High	50	58·0	25	52·0
Medium	22	59·1	33	48·5
Low	53	60·4	64	56·2

continued overleaf

	P4 Good Readers		P4 Poor Readers	
	N pupils	Per cent who deteriorate	N pupils	Per cent who improve
6. Home encouragement: Satisfactory	206	31·6	129	51·9**
Poor	8	37·5	78	26·9**
7. School attendance: Satisfactory	211	32·0	189	42·9
Poor	4	25·0	20	35·0
8. School type: Grant-aided†	63	12·5	—	—
Public: Roman Catholic	31	29·0	51	33·2
Non-denom.	197	32·5	172	44·3

Notes: †63 pupils attending grant-aided schools excluded from main sample and subsequent cross tabulations on account of their unrepresentative social and intellectual background.
*Statistical significance ≤ ·05 ⎫
**Statistical significance ≤ ·01 ⎭ (two-tailed chi² test).

Table 9.3: Progress of good and poor readers between primary 4 and primary 7: related to out-of-school reading

	P4 Good readers		P4 Poor readers	
	n pupils	Per cent who deteriorate	n pupils	Per cent who improve
Total sample	228	32·0	223	41·7
1. Books mentioned in P4:				
Two or more titles	111	22·5**	42	64·3**
One title	67	41·8**	77	36·4**
None mentioned	31	45·2**	68	33·8**
2. Comics, magazines or newspapers mentioned in P4:				
Four or more	91	26·4	33	60·6*
Two or three	71	35·2	40	50·0*
One or none	50	36·0	112	34·8*

3. Changes in out-of-school reading		P4 Good readers		P4 Poor readers	
P4	P6	n pupils	Per cent who deteriorate	n pupils	Per cent who improve
2 or more books	2 or more books	61	18·0*	—	—
	1 or no books	33	30·3*	—	—
1 or more books	2 or more books	42	33·3*	—	—
	1 or no books	45	48·9*	—	—
1 or more books	1 or more books	—	—	53	56·6*
	No books	—	—	48	35·4*
No books	1 or more books	—	—	23	39·1
	No books	—	—	30	30·0

Note: *Statistical significance ≤ ·05 (one-tailed chi²).

Table 9.4: Progress of good and poor readers between primary 4 and primary 7 related to practices and attitudes of class teachers over three sessions

	P4 Good readers		P4 Poor readers	
		Per cent		Per cent
	n	who	n	who
	pupils	deteriorate	pupils	improve
Total sample	228	32·0	223	41·7
1. Use of reading labs in:				
All three sessions	120	25·9	77	44·2
One or two sessions	50	31·7	86	43·0
Never used	58	35·0	60	36·7
2. Use of textbooks for activities other than English or maths in:				
All three sessions	45	28·9	70	32·9*
One or two sessions	70	37·1	80	40·0*
Never used	113	30·1	73	52·1*
3. Homework provisions (2+ sessions):				
Prescribed reading	52	28·8	93	42·0
Other provisions	102	28·4	92	37·0
No homework	74	37·8	38	42·1
4. Use of comics in class (2+ sessions):				
Permitted	70	31·4	80	48·8*
Discouraged	68	33·8	95	29·2*
Varied	88	31·8	48	42·1*
5. Supply of books in school (2+ sessions):				
Satisfactory	100	32·0	106	47·2*
Unsatisfactory	38	42·1	49	55·1*
Mixed views	90	27·8	68	23·5*
6. Nature of reading:				
Enjoyment and information	79	24·1	82	37·8
Skill and comprehension	80	33·8	63	42·9
Multiple responses	62	40·3	74	47·3
7. Reasons for achievement differences:				
Home background	55	41·8*	67	37·3
Intelligence	34	26·5 } *	27	37·0
Multiple responses	133	28·6 }	118	44·9

Table 9.5: Progress of good and poor readers between primary 4 and primary 7: related to miscellaneous classroom factors

	P4 Good readers		P4 Poor readers	
	n pupils	*Per cent who deteriorate*	*n pupils*	*Per cent who improve*
Total sample	228	32·0	223	41·7
1. Average reading attainment of class in P4:				
Above average	86	34·9	14	35·7
Average	118	31·4	97	43·3
Below average	19	26·3	106	37·7
2. Pupil turnover in class between P4 and P7:				
Over 50%	40	35·2	51	34·6*
25–50%	82	28·6	86	40·2 ⎫ *
Below 25%	37	32·2	40	51·2 ⎭
3. Length of teachers' experience (2+ sessions):				
Over 5 years	56	33·1	22	42·9
2–5 years	44	27·3	69	39·1
Under 2 years	26	42·3	48	43·8
Varied	102	31·4	84	40·9
4. Class composition (2+ sessions):				
Single age group	129	30·2	145	40·7
Mixed age group	99	30·7	78	43·8

Chapter 10

From Primary to Secondary School:

A Follow-up of Good and Poor Readers

Graham F. Atherton

In the previous chapter socioeconomic background and the amount of reading done out of school were shown to have cumulative effects on the reading progress of pupils moving from their fourth to final year of primary school. A parallel investigation was conducted among pupils identified as good or poor readers in primary 7 classes, who were then retested in their third year of secondary school. Of particular interest was the question whether socioeconomic background and out of school reading activities would continue to affect reading progress in secondary school as much as in primary school. A related issue was whether transfer to secondary education was attended by a change in the amount and type of reading done out of school.

Stage 3 of the Edinburgh Reading Test was completed in autumn 1972 by 2517 pupils in primary 7 classes, of whom 477 were classified as good readers and 424 classified as poor readers, their test scores falling one standard deviation above or below the sample mean, respectively. By the time pupils were again tested three years later, there was a 30 per cent loss of pupils identified as good or poor readers. The losses were greater among the poor readers, who were more likely to be found in areas of urban depopulation and secondary reorganization. Their absence rate was probably also higher. It was nevertheless possible to determine to what extent pupils identified as good or poor readers in primary 7 either maintained or departed from their relative position on completing the test in secondary 3. More than 56 per cent of good readers had 'deteriorated' and only 25 per cent of poor readers had 'improved' between test sessions. These somewhat alarming changes in reading standards should be seen as relative shifts over time, not as absolute differences in performance; they refer to changes in relative attainment of pupils in one test sample compared with another. The fact remains, however, that more than half of the primary 7 good readers no longer occupied the top 16 per cent of the test distribution when retested three years later. There was no evidence that the good readers were being displaced by higher achievers who were added to the original sample between test sessions; 'newcomers' were of similar mean attainment to the core sample completing both tests. But as with the younger test cohort (moving from primary 4 to primary 7), statistical regression effects arising from test-retest unreliability would be expected to account for some of the deterioration and improvement.

Reading progress

Table 10.1 describes how reading progress between primary 7 and secondary 3 was related to various group factors. The most noticeable feature in the table was the greater influence of social environment on the progress of the good readers than of the poor readers, contradicting the notion that cumulative disadvantage is something which affects the low rather than the high achievers. Good readers who had attended a primary school of low socioeconomic status, as assessed by 1971 census indices, or whose fathers were employed in semi- or unskilled occupations showed far more relative deterioration compared with good readers from higher social backgrounds (Tables 10.1.2 and 10.1.3). But social background was not related to the progress of the poor readers to such a high or consistent degree. Indeed, poor readers from semi- and unskilled backgrounds showed a slightly higher incidence of improvement compared with poor readers from other backgrounds. It would appear that once primary schooling has been completed, parents of non-manual status are prepared to offer encouragement to read only if their children are already doing well and are less inclined to do so if they are performing badly. The only factor that readily predicted subsequent performance of the poor readers was the level of encouragement received in the home as perceived by the primary 7 class teacher (Table 10.1.5). Only 12 per cent of poor readers from homes judged as unsatisfactory showed some improvement in their reading by the time they reached secondary 3. Teachers' perceptions of individual pupils appear to be far more important than socioeconomic status in assessing the potential of poor readers. The most advantaged members of the sample were good readers attending grant-aided schools, who were far less likely to fall behind in their reading than even children of professional and managerial backgrounds attending education authority schools (Table 10.1.7).

Next consideration was given to the amount of reading children did out of school hours and its relation to reading progress between test sessions. Pupils reported the names of any books, comics, or magazines they had read in the previous seven days in a questionnaire completed by them in primary 7 and secondary 2. Results are presented in Table 10.2. Perhaps surprisingly, the number of books mentioned was not a particularly important predictor of progress between primary 7 and secondary 3. Both good and poor readers who had mentioned two books or more in primary 7 showed an incidence of deterioration or improvement in reading that was hardly different from progress achieved by pupils who had mentioned no books at all (Table 10.2.1). Only in the earlier stages of schooling, between primary 4 and primary 7, was the amount of book reading positively related to progress. By the time pupils reach the end of primary school, the benefits derived from reading books at home have reached saturation point as far as standardized reading test attainment is concerned.

However, this was not entirely the case with non-fiction, newspaper and magazine reading, which continued to be related to progress even beyond primary school. Good readers whose out-of-school reading in primary 7 included some non-fiction books and at least three newspapers or magazines showed less deterioration than good readers not mentioning these items. Greater improvement was also observed among poor readers who had read three or more newspapers or magazines (Tables 10.3.3. and 10.3.4). Progress was further enhanced where out of school reading was accompanied by a low level of comic consumption, good readers who had mentioned no comics in primary 7 showing a much lower incidence of deterioration by secondary 3.

Changes in reading habits between primary 7 and secondary 2 were also examined. Pupils mentioning the names of more books in secondary 2 than in primary 7 showed little more progress than pupils whose book reading had not increased but there was slightly less deterioration in performance among good readers who were reading more non-fiction in secondary 2 relative to primary 7. Good readers who reported a higher ratio of newspaper and magazine reading to comic reading in secondary 2 compared with primary 7 also made greater strides forward. The nature of the changes in out-of-school reading habits will now be described in more detail.

Out of school reading
There was evidence of a considerable shift in the quantity and quality of out of school reading as pupils moved from primary 7 to

secondary 2. On average good readers mentioned fewer books in secondary 2 than in primary 7, though poor readers reported about the same number of books as before (Table 10.3). Among the good readers, girls were much more likely than boys to be reading fewer books as they moved into secondary school, boys mentioning only slightly fewer books in secondary 2 than in primary 7. Socioeconomic background also played a strong part in determining how many books were read. Good readers who had attended primary schools of high socioeconomic status or whose fathers were employed in non-manual occupations were reading more books than were good readers of lower social background by the time they reached secondary 2 (Tables 10.3.2 and 10.3.3). Good readers of lower socioeconomic background were more likely to cut down on books as they grew older. Socioeconomic factors had little influence on the number of books read by poor readers, who mentioned only about a third as many titles as the good readers in both primary 7 and secondary 2.

The largest number of book titles was mentioned by good readers attending grant-aided schools, while poor readers in Roman Catholic schools were mentioning more books than poor readers in non-denominational schools (Table 10.3.5). Finally, good readers who had been taught in primary 7 classes of below average reading attainment were reading fewer books in both primary and secondary school than good readers originating from classes of higher attainment.

Children's fiction and non-fiction reading habits were then analysed separately. Fiction was much more popular than non-fiction, both among good and poor readers, but both types of reading were subject to a decline as pupils entered secondary schooling. In primary 7, over 80 per cent of good readers and 48 per cent of poor readers mentioned some fiction books; in secondary 2, there proportions fell to 72 per cent and 34 per cent. Non-fiction titles were mentioned by 59 per cent of good readers and 23 per cent of poor readers in primary 7; but by secondary 2, non-fiction was read by 51 per cent of good readers and 20 per cent of poor readers. These changes mask important group differences, however. For example, there was a much more drastic curtailment of non-fiction reading among girls than boys. In primary 7, 51 per cent of the girls who were also good readers mentioned some non-fiction titles, but by secondary 2, only 32 per cent did so. Boys, on the other hand, mentioned about as much non-fiction in secondary 2 as in primary 7. There was a higher incidence of non-fiction reading among good readers of non-manual background or who were attending grant-aided schools; these pupils were less likely to restrict their non-fiction reading as they moved to secondary school, compared with good readers of lower social background. Nearly three-quarters of them mentioned some non-fiction titles in secondary 2, compared with 45 per cent of good readers of manual background doing so.

The incidence of non-fiction reading among the poor readers was also affected by socioeconomic background to some extent. A third of poor readers of non-manual background were reading some non-fiction in secondary 2, compared with only 16 per cent from manual backgrounds, differences which were not evident in primary 7.

The move from primary to secondary school was marked by a decline in comic consumption and an increase in newspaper and magazine reading, particularly among the good readers. As Tables 10.4 and 10.5 indicate, good readers mentioned more comics than newspapers or magazines in primary 7, but by secondary 2, the position was reversed, with newspapers and magazines outnumbering comics. Poor readers also stepped up their consumption of newspapers and magazines as they moved into secondary school, although the average number of titles they mentioned was still well less than half of that mentioned by the good readers, and they were still reading more comics than newspapers or magazines.

Cutbacks in comic consumption were by no means uniform across social groups. Among the good readers, boys were much more likely than girls to read fewer comics as they got older. Boys mentioned half the number of titles in secondary 2 as in primary 7, whereas the girls mentioned virtually the same number at both stages in their schooling. Among the poor readers, boys in secondary 2 were reading half as many comics as the girls, who were actually reading more comics in secondary school than in primary school. It was not possible to distinguish between different types of comic, but the greater inclination of girls to read comics up to a later age compared with boys could be connected with the proliferation of comic-strips oriented to teenage pop and romance. There was also an association between father's occupation and comic consumption. Among the good readers, pupils of skilled manual origin mentioned more comics than those from either non-manual or semi- and unskilled backgrounds, while among the poor readers, pupils from non-manual background read fewer comics than manual pupils (Table 10.4.3). The smallest number of comics mentioned came from pupils attending grant-aided secondary schools, and there was a very sharp decline in comic consumption among good readers in Roman Catholic schools.

There were also some interesting patterns in newspaper and magazine reading as pupils transferred from primary to secondary school. The number of titles mentioned did not differ greatly between boys and girls, and both groups increased their consumption as they moved into secondary school (Table 10.5).

There were some important socioeconomic differences in newspaper and magazine reading habits. As pupils moved to secondary school, socioeconomic differences in the number of titles mentioned by the good readers became more divergent, but among the poor readers, socioeconomic differences converged. Good readers who had attended primary schools of low socioeconomic status or who came from semi- and unskilled backgrounds were reading about the same number of newspapers or magazines as good readers from higher social backgrounds in their final year of primary school. But on reaching secondary 2, they mentioned considerably fewer titles than the latter group. On the other hand, poor readers from manual backgrounds were reading fewer newspapers and magazines than their non-manual counterparts in primary 7, whereas in secondary 2, a similar number of items was mentioned by both groups (Tables 10.4.2 and 10.4.3). The highest consumption of all was reported among good readers attending grant-aided schools, and there was a large increase among poor readers moving to Roman Catholic secondary schools. Pupils who had been taught in primary school classes of average or above average reading attainment were also likely to be reading more newspapers or magazines as they moved into secondary school, compared with pupils originating from classes of lower attainment.

Verbal reasoning quotient

Verbal reasoning quotients were obtained for pupils who completed stage 3 of the Reading Test in autumn 1972. Pupils who had been classified as good readers had a mean VRQ of 112·8 and poor readers a mean VRQ of 83·6, with standard deviations of 9·5 and 7·5 respectively. There were no significant sex or social class differences in VRQ within each of the good and poor groups. Pupils attending schools in Glasgow were excluded from the tabulations. VRQ, being highly correlated with Reading quotient, was, not surprisingly, a good predictor of reading progress as pupils moved from primary 7 to secondary 3. Some 46 per cent of good readers with a VRQ above the group median (114) deteriorated in performance compared with 64 per cent of good readers with VRQs below the median. Likewise, 39 per cent of poor readers with VRQs above the group median (83) improved in performance compared with only 13 per cent with VRQs below the median doing as well.

Conclusions

Over half of the good readers and three-quarters of the poor readers failed to make any progress in their reading status as they moved from primary to secondary school. Good readers coming from low social backgrounds and poor readers receiving little encouragement at home were particularly at risk. Progress was not so strongly affected by the amount of reading done out of school, whose benefits were more evident during the earlier stages of schooling, but children who were reading more newspapers or magazines and fewer comics were likely to fare better. Good readers mentioned the titles of fewer books as they moved from primary to secondary school, especially girls and pupils from manual backgrounds, but the poor readers continued to read the same number of books as before. Fiction was much more popular than non-fiction, with the girls mentioning less non-fiction as they got older. Girls were also reading comics up to a later age compared with boys. Both good and poor readers reported an increase in newspapers and magazine consumption as they moved to secondary school. The average reading attainment of the primary 7 class attended was a positive indicator of the amount of reading done out of school.

Table 10.1: Progress of good and poor readers between primary 7 and secondary 2: socioeconomic factors

	P7 Good readers		P7 Poor readers	
		Per cent		Per cent
	n	who	n	who
	pupils	deteriorate	pupils	improve
Total sample	267	56·9	250	25·6
1. Sex: Boys	142	52·1	119	21·0
Girls	125	62·4	130	29·2
2. School socioeconomic status: High	105	47·1*	40	32·5
Medium	51	55·2*	69	21·7
Low	53	64·2*	94	20·2
3. Father's occupation: Non-manual	95	45·3*	27	25·9
Skilled manual	112	58·8*	101	22·8
Semi/Unskilled Manual	51	64·3*	98	30·6

continued overleaf

		P7 Good readers		P7 Poor readers	
			Per cent		Per cent
		n	who	n	who
4. School socioeconomic status:		pupils	deteriorate	pupils	improve
(i) Non-manual pupils:	High	53	47·2	7	28·6
	Medium	23	34·8	8	25·0
	Low	8	37·5	8	12·5
(ii) Manual pupils:	High	49	63·2	30	30·0
	Medium	27	55·5	55	23·7
	Low	42	69·0	75	21·3
5. Home encouragement:	Satisfactory	240	55·8	131	35·1*
	Poor	8	37·5	90	12·2*
6. School attendance in Primary 7:					
	Satisfactory	233	54·9	189	25·4
	Poor	2	—	20	18·2
7. School type:					
	Grant-aided[1]	107	32·7*	—	—
	Public: R.C.	55	60·6*	40	37·5
	Non-denominational	212	56·1*	210	23·3
8. Reading attainment of P7 class:					
	Above average	107	53·3	29	24·1
	Average	124	58·1	104	23·1
	Below average	33	60·6	109	27·5

Chi^2 test: Percentage difference significant at ·05 level (*).
[1]Pupils attending two grant-aided schools in the survey excluded from all other tabulations.

Table 10.2: Progress of good and poor readers between primary 7 and secondary 3: out-of-school reading

		P7 Good readers		P7 Poor readers	
			Per cent		Per cent
		n	who	n	who
		pupils	deteriorate	pupils	improve
Total Sample		267	56·9	250	25·6
Titles mentioned in P7					
1. Books:	Two or more	137	57·7	26	34·6
	One only	53	56·6	86	20·9
	None	24	62·5	89	28·1
2. Fiction:	One or more	196	55·1	95	24·2
	None	47	63·8	110	30·0
3. Non-fiction:	One or more	149	53·7*	48	25·0
	None	92	60·9*	153	26·1
4. Newspapers/periodicals:	Three or more	62	50·0*	15	40·0*
	One or two	97	61·9*	61	32·8*
	None	54	61·1*	125	20·8*
5. Comics:	Three or more	104	60·6*	58	29·3
	One or two	84	59·5*	92	26·1
	None	26	42·3*	51	21·6

Table 10.3: Out-of-school reading activities among primary 7 good and poor readers moving to secondary 2

		P7 Good readers Average number of titles mentioned in:		P7 Poor readers Average number of titles mentioned in:	
		P7	S2	P7	S2
Books:	Total Sample	2·2	1·9	0·7	0·7
1.	Sex: Boys	2·2	2·1	0·6	0·6
	Girls	2·3	1·7	0·8	0·8
2.	School SES: High	2·2	2·1	0·7	0·5
	Medium	2·0	1·5	0·6	0·3
	Low	2·1	1·8	0·6	0 8
3.	Father's Occupation:				
	Non-manual	2·3	2·2	0·9	0·9
	Skilled manual	2·1	1·7	0·7	0·6
	Semi-skilled	2·1	1·7	0·8	0·8
4.	Home Encouragement:				
	Satisfactory	2·2	1·8	0·8	0·7
	Poor	—	—	0·7	0·5
5.	School Type:				
	Grant-aided[1]	2·8	2·7	—	—
	Roman Catholic	2·4	2·0	1·0*	1·0*
	Other	2·1	1·9	0·7*	0·6*
6.	Reading attain of P7 class:				
	Above average	2·3	2·0	0·7	0·5
	Average	2·2	2·0	0·7	0·8
	Below average	1·7	1·5	0·7	0·6

F ratio mean differences within columns (*) significant at ·05 level.
[1] Pupils attending the two grant-aided schools in the survey excluded from all other tabulations.

Table 10.4: Out-of-school reading activities among primary 7 good and poor readers moving to secondary 2

		P7 Good readers Average number of titles mentioned in:		P7 Poor readers Average number of titles mentioned in:	
		P7	S2	P7	S2
Comics:	Total Sample	3·0	2·2	1·8	1·9
1.	Sex: Boys	2·9	1·6***	1·6*	1·3*
	Girls	3·1	3·0***	2·0*	2·5*
2.	School SES: High	2·7	2·2 ⎫ *	1·6	1·7
	Medium	3·0	2·1 ⎭	1·9	1·9
	Low	3·0	2·9*	1·8	2·1

continued overleaf

		P7 Good readers Average number of titles mentioned in:		P7 Poor readers Average number of titles mentioned in:	
		P7	S2	P7	S2
3.	Father's Occupation:				
	Non-manual	2·7*	1·8*	1·6	1·4*
	Skilled manual	3·4*	2·6*	1·9	2·1 ⎱ *
	Semi-unskilled	2·4*	2·0*	1·8	2·0 ⎰
4.	Home encouragement:				
	Satisfactory	2·9	2·1*	1·9	1·7
	Unsatisfactory	—	—	1·6	2·0
5.	School type: Grant-aided[1]	2·2*	0·8*	—	—
	Roman Catholic	3·5*	1·6*	2·1	1·9
	Other	2·8*	2·4*	1·8	1·9
6.	Reading attainment of P7 class:				
	Above average	3·0	2·1	2·0	1·7
	Average	3·0	2·2	1·9	1·8
	Below average	2·8	2·3	1·8	1·9

F-ratio: Mean difference within column (*) significant at ·05 level.
[1] Pupils attending the two grant-aided schools in the survey excluded from all other tabulations.

Table 10.5: Newspapers and periodicals

		P7 Good readers Average number of titles mentioned in:		P7 Poor readers Average number of titles mentioned in:	
		P7	S2	P7	S2
	Total Sample	1·7	2·9	0·6	1·2
1.	Sex: Boys	1·8	3·0	0·7	1·1
	Girls	1·6	2·8	0·7	1·4
2.	School SES: High	1·4	3·0 ⎱ *	0·5	0·9
	Medium	2·0	2·9 ⎰	0·6	1·0
	Low	1·6	2·5*	0·7*	1·2
3.	Father's Occupation:				
	Non-manual	1·6	3·1 ⎱ *	1·0*	1·0
	Skilled manual	1·9	2·9 ⎰	0·6*	1·3
	Semi-unskilled	1·6	2·5*	0·6	1·1
4.	Home encouragement:				
	Satisfactory	1·7	3·0*	0·7	1·4*
	Poor	—	—	0·5	1·0*
5.	School type: Grant-aided[1]	2·4*	3·3	—	—
	Roman Catholic	1·8 ⎱ *	2·8	0·6	2·2*
	Other	1·7 ⎰	3·2	0·6	1·0*
6.	Reading attainment of P7 class:				
	Above average	1·4	2·9 ⎱ *	0·3*	0·6*
	Average	1·8	3·0 ⎰	0·8*	1·5*
	Below average	2·0	2·5*	0·6*	1·2*

F-ratio: Mean difference within column (*) significant at ·05 level.
[1] Pupils attending the two grant-aided schools in the survey excluded from all other tabulations.

Chapter 11

Remedial Reading

Remedy: v.   to cure (a disease etc); to put right, reform (a state of things); to rectify, make good.

Remedial: adj. affording a remedy, tending to relieve or redress.

Oxford English Dictionary

Despite the dictionary, there is no clear definition of 'remedial' as applied to pupils or classes in either primary or secondary schools. The situation is, to put it mildly, confused. Whether pupils receive remedial teaching or not appeared to depend on teachers' judgment of how backward pupils were and what facilities for remedial teaching were available at the time. Presentation of the current practices and provisions for remedial teaching is further complicated by the fact that over the years covered by this investigation, provision for remedial teaching was fluctuating, and by the fact that as pupils progressed through primary school the incidence of remedial teaching tended to increase up to P4, and decrease from P4 to P7. In view of the lack of uniform provision and established definition, a systematic presentation of remedial facilities and practices within schools would be misleading. In the discussion that follows, the term 'remedial' has been used for those pupils who are receiving special teaching over and above that provided within the class by the class teacher. This remedial teaching is normally done by a visiting or residential remedial teacher, or by a member of the school staff other than the class teacher. Though remedial teaching was not necessarily confined to reading, in practice nearly all pupils classed as remedial were receiving some sort of tuition in reading.

Provisions for remedial teaching in primary schools

An extensive national survey into provisions for remedial teaching was made by the (SCCOPE) Scottish Central Committee on Primary Education[1], and it was not thought necessary to duplicate this in detail for the schools in the present investigation. None of the data obtained here are incompatible with the SCCOPE findings. The present investigation began in session 1972/3, and teachers in P4 and P7 classes were asked to identify the pupils receiving remedial education. It became evident that remedial teaching depended as much on facilities available as pupils' needs and more detailed information was obtained for the following school sessions. In 1974/5, all schools were asked for returns for all primary classes, and the data obtained are set out in Table 11.1.

Table 11.1: Incidence of remedial teaching by classes

	P1	P2	P3	P4	P5	P6	P7
No. schools giving remedial teaching	10	18	31	36	33	28	26
No. pupils receiving remedial teaching	54	94	188	248	172	134	104

In this sample school session, it appears that the peak incidence of remedial teaching is in the P4 classes. Some schools did not provide remedial facilities for P1 and P2 classes, and others ceased remedial teaching after P6. Though policies varied, the above figures give a fairly representative picture of school practice.

The changes in provisions for the classes whose progress has been surveyed in this report are shown in Table 11.2.

Table 11.2: Remedial provisions by classes P4 to P7

	1972/3		1973/4	1974/5
	P4	P7	P5	P6
No. schools with rem. pupils	30	13	37	30
No. pupils receiving remedial teaching	141	41	213	134

The apparent deficiency in remedial pupils in P4, P5 and P7 is due to the fact that between 1972/3 and 1974/5, not only had the number of schools with remedial provisions increased, but also the provisions in schools already supplied had expanded.

---

[1] Scottish Central Committee on Primary Education, *Remedial Education in Primary School* – A Survey: Jan. 1974.

Pupils receiving remedial teaching were withdrawn from their classes either individually or in small groups. The average time per week spent by pupils at remedial tuition was 0·6 hours, or 36 minutes. This is an average value and only summarizes a wide variety of practices, from almost daily attendances of about 20 minutes in some schools, to longer sessions, sometimes at monthly intervals in schools served by visiting remedial specialists. It proved impossible to identify any substantially common practice.

The procedure by which a pupil was referred for remedial teaching also varied. The practices set out in the SCCOPE report were largely reflected in the practices in the schools in this investigation. In 95 per cent of the schools with remedial provision the class teacher was involved in the decisions to refer for remedial teaching, in 72 per cent, the head or assistant head was involved, in 35 per cent the remedial teacher was involved and in 16 per cent the school psychological services were involved. In general, therefore, the decision to refer a pupil for remedial teaching was taken by the class and head teachers.

The procedure for return to normal class teaching was somewhat similar. In 63 per cent of the schools, the class teacher was involved, in 38 per cent the head or assistant head teacher was involved, in 78 per cent, the remedial teacher was involved and in 13 per cent the school psychologist was involved. The percentages for referral are based on 75 schools, and for returns on 60 schools. Finally, in P5 and P6 classes, 38 class teachers considered the coordination between remedial and normal class teaching to be satisfactory, and 20 considered it unsatisfactory. The latter figure does not include some ten or so teachers who preferred to do their own remedial teaching within the classroom, rather than refer to a specialist.

Diagnosis of reading difficulties

Only a minority of the remedial teachers had received formal training by in-service courses designed for that purpose. The others were retired teachers or other part-time teachers, or a member of school staff with particular interest or experience in reading, who undertook some remedial work in addition to other school duties. As 43 per cent of the 141 pupils recorded as receiving remedial teaching in P4 continued to receive remedial teaching in P5, and 23 per cent continued to receive remedial teaching in P5 and P6, there is about a quarter of the P4 remedial pupils in continuous attendance for remedial tuition over a period of three years. In addition there is another 14 per cent who were considered to need further remedial teaching, but who for various reasons, mainly lack of available remedial teachers, were not receiving it. In short there are 37 per cent of the original P4 remedial pupils who were either receiving or were needing remedial attention over a span of three years of their primary education.

To maintain even a quarter of the P4 remedial pupils in remedial classes for three years involves considerable development of teacher time and effort, and raises the question not only of the effectiveness of the teaching methods, but also of the original diagnosis.

In this investigation, the average reading quotient of pupils receiving remedial teaching was just below RQ=80, and of all the 438 pupils recorded as receiving remedial teaching in P4, P5 and P6, only 4 had reading quotients of RQ=100 or over. The figures indicate that pupils are selected for remedial teaching by comparison of their reading standards with those of the other pupils in the class, those of unacceptably low standard being referred. This was confirmed in discussions with class and head teachers. The alternative criterion for selection, comparison of the pupils' current standard of reading with the best estimate of their possible standard was scarcely ever used. The result appears to be that remedial teaching is confined to pupils clearly below average reading attainment.

The remedial groups, therefore, contain an assortment of pupils with different disabilities. There are those of a low level of intellectual ability who are probably reading as well as they can, those whose reading difficulties may be presenting symptoms of more serious emotional disturbance, those whose difficulties arise from prolonged absence or incompatible teaching methods, those who suffer from a number of specific disabilities, which may or may not be wholly or partly remediable, those whose attainment may be unacceptably low in the classes of higher average reading attainment, but would have been acceptable in classes of below average attainment, and those who suffer from any combination of such disabilities. In the absence of adequate diagnosis it is not possible to establish the incidence of these different sources of reading disability. Three pupils were reported as suffering from dyslexia, and though the investigators were not competent to reach a firm diagnosis, it seemed fairly clear that one was not, one probably was not, and the third probably was. But no record could be found of a pupil referred for remedial teaching who had been adequately examined for hearing or similar perceptual defects. It is also fairly clear on the face of it that where about 90 per cent of the referrals were made by class or head teachers, that detailed and competent assessment of the pupils disabilities were not made, despite the fact that at least a quarter of the pupils were to occupy the time and attention of a remedial teacher for the next three years.

The conspicuous absence of pupils of average or above average reading attainment in the remedial group again indicates inadequate diagnosis for it does not seem impossible that there are pupils whose level of reading attainment is acceptable to the class teacher, but who may have some disability which prevents them from attaining a higher standard of performance. Though teachers may have some difficulty in deciding whether such pupils justify use of remedial teaching resources, the fact that they are not adequately identified in practice relieves the teacher of the need to make such a decision. Also it is possible for pupils to have developed what might paradoxically be described as an unacceptably high level of reading performance, and are able to develop more advanced reading skills than their contemporaries. If it is one of the functions of the remedial services to relieve the class teacher of those pupils whose abilities fall clearly outwith the normal range of differences with a class, then the case for special attention for the more advanced pupils is parallel to that for the more backward pupils.

Diagnosis of reading deficiencies is not easy. If the function of remedial teaching is to relieve or assist the class teacher in teaching the pupils who do not fit easily into the pattern of normal class teaching, the initial identification of such pupils would properly be made by the class and head teacher. In the system as it at present exists, the appropriate reference would appear to be to the school psychological services, rather than direct to the remedial teacher. In only about 15 per cent of the schools was the psychologist involved. The assessment of the pupils would be expected usually to include medical and social opinion as well as psychological, to avoid the likelihood of pupils suffering from, for example, emotional disturbance or sensory defect having their difficulties remedied by being taught to read. If, on the other hand, the proper function of remedial teaching is to relate the pupils' reading attainments as closely as possible to their abilities, the need for adequate diagnosis is equally great. The assessment of a pupil's potential is far from easy, but some estimate can be made. The class teacher must again be the starting point in identification of pupils requiring remedial attention, and parents can assist. The making of the best estimate of what a pupil can do, in comparison with what the pupil is doing, is subject to error, but can be attempted. There appeared in this inquiry little awareness on the part of class teachers that such identification for remedial teaching could apply to pupils of acceptable reading competence as well as those whose standard of reading was below acceptable level. Again, the expertise of the school psychologists was not frequently called on.

The procedure for return of pupils to full-time normal class teaching seems equally haphazard, and is often determined by availability of staff and pressure of new referrals. Even when these conditions are absent, there is little evidence of thorough assessment of the pupils' progress. In most cases it seems to be a decision by the remedial teacher.

Whether the greater call on diagnostic services would be balanced by a saving resulting from greater effectiveness of the remedial services is not a question that can be answered by this inquiry. There does emerge from the investigation a need for a more thorough examination of the operation of remedial teaching services, particularly in the selection of pupils, the assessment of their progress, the relationship between class and remedial teaching, and the procedures whereby pupils either continue to receive remedial teaching or are returned to full-time class teaching.

The reading progress of pupils receiving remedial teaching

The methods and materials used in remedial groups was not investigated in detail. The main reason was that remedial teaching was, or should be, by its nature individual, suited to the needs and abilities of each pupil. General practices, as opposed to individual attention, should not prevail. Also, investigation was concerned with the teaching of reading to all pupils, and the teachers' practices in teaching pupils of average or above average ability is as of great, if not of more importance than methods used in teaching pupils whose progress was slower than that of their contemporaries.

It is possible, however, to make some assessment of the relative progress and attainment of those pupils classed as remedial. Of the 141 pupils in P4 designated remedial, 130 have scores on Edinburgh Reading Test Stage 2. The mean Raw Score for these 130 pupils was 9·3 points, the mean for the 78 boys being 10·0 (sd=9·5) and for the 52 girls the mean was 8·3 (sd=6·9). Of these 130 remedial pupils tested in P4, 81 sat the Edinburgh Reading Test Stage 3 in P7 three years later. It is on the basis of these 81 pupils that comparisons can be made.

The P4 and P7 pupils took different reading tests, Stage 2 and Stage 3 respectively, so no direct assessment of amount of progress is possible.

All P4 pupils in the sample had mean Stage 2 score of RS$=26$ (SD$=20$) and all P7 pupils had a mean Stage 3 score of RS$=84$ (SD$=35$). The difference of 58 points is given here only as a basis for comparison with the progress of the 81 remedial pupils in P4 who were also tested in P7. The mean P4 score for these pupils was RS$=8\cdot5$ (SD$=7\cdot2$), and the mean P7 score was RS$=44\cdot3$ (SD$=22\cdot8$). The difference of 36 points is less than that for all pupils, but that is all that can be said. The skew distribution of P4 scores makes comparison in SD units doubtful.

However, a comparison can be made within the 81 pupils. There are 21 of them who received remedial teaching in P4, P5 and P6, called RRR, and 14, called ROO, who received no further remedial teaching in P5 or P6. Test Scores are as below:

Raw Score	Mean P4	SD P4	Mean P7	SD P7	No.
RRR	10·6	9·0	37·1	20·8	21
ROO	8·4	6·0	57·7	29·2	14

A corresponding table can be constructed taking those P4 remedial pupils who were tested in both P5 and P7, where scores can be expressed as Reading Quotients.

Reading Quotient	Mean P5	Mean P7	No.
RRR	78·4	77·8	25
ROO	86·9	89·0	11

The raw scores are difficult to interpret. The two groups RRR and ROO began at approximately the same level of attainment, but those who continued to receive remedial teaching reached a significantly lower level of attainment in P7 than those who did not. In the Reading Quotient tables, the differences between RRR and ROO groups are significant both for P5 and P7, but in neither group are the differences between P5 RQs and P7 RQs either large or significant. The RRR and ROO groups both fail to make progress, relative to their contemporaries between P5 and P7, though remaining at different levels of attainment.

A more comprehensive record is available for remedial pupils recorded as such in the P5 classes. There are 287 pupils (117 boys and 110 girls) recorded as needing remedial teaching in P5. These include the P4 remedials continuing to receive remedial teaching in P5, which can further be divided into two groups, one of 161 pupils receiving remedial teaching in their schools, and 126 pupils considered by their schools to need remedial teaching, but who were not receiving it. The mean RQ in P5 of the first group was RQ=79·5 and of the second RQ=79·4. The attainment level of the two groups is identical, suggesting remedial teaching is based on provisions available rather than on pupil need.

From these 287 pupils, two groups of 54 and 16 pupils were followed through P6 and their P7 RQs recorded. The two groups are called RR and NN, the first receiving remedial teaching in both P5 and P6, and the second needing but not receiving in both P5 and P6. The latter group received any special teaching there was, from their class teachers. The RQs of the two groups are given below.

Reading Quotients	Mean P5	Mean P7	No.
RR	80·0	78·2	54
NN	76·8	74·6	16

The apparent drop in mean RQ from P5 to P7 can be ignored; it is the result of test standardization, and in both groups the P5 and P7 mean RQs can be taken as identical. Neither group has progressed between P5 and P7 relative to their contemporaries; their status in the sample has remained the same. None of the differences between RR and NN or between P5 and P7 is significant statistically.

What should be a matter for concern is that there emerges no difference in progress between two similar groups of pupils, where one is receiving two years of remedial teaching, and the other none. This suggests that much of the work of the remedial teacher of reading could be done, and is being done, equally well by the class teacher.

Progress of P7 remedial pupils in secondary schools

Of the 41 pupils recorded as receiving remedial teaching in P7 in session 1972/3, 40 took the Edinburgh Reading Test Stage 3, obtaining a mean RQ=77·4 (SD=8·6). Of these, 33 had also scores on the Verbal Reasoning Test (Moray House 74). For these 33 pupils, mean RQ=76·4 (SD=7·3) and mean VRQ=77·3 (SD=5·6). Correlation between RQ and VRQ gives $r=+0·5$. The group of 40 pupils contained 25 boys (mean RQ=79·2) and 15 girls (mean RQ=74·3).

Of the 40 pupils with P7 test scores, 38 proceeded to eight secondary schools, 33 to five schools with mixed ability classes, and 5 to three schools which contained smaller remedial classes, with average size of 15 pupils. The five schools operated remedial teaching on the withdrawal system.

By Sec 3, only 24 of the pupils were recorded as having taken the reading test, 11 taking Stage 3, 11 taking Stage 4 and 2 taking both. The 13 pupils with scores on Stage 3 in both P7 and Sec 3 had in P7, a mean RS$=44\cdot9$ (SD$=24\cdot0$) and in Sec 3 a mean RS$=57\cdot1$ (SD$=16\cdot7$). The difference in raw score is a direct measure of their improvement. Compared with the average difference of 31·8 points of score for all pupils repeating Stage 3 of the test (see Chapter 7), the difference of 12·2 points for the P7 remedial pupils is small. It is clear that these pupils have not improved as much as their contemporaries.

The mean reading quotient of these 24 pupils in P7 was RQ$=77\cdot2$ (SD$=9\cdot5$) and in Sec 3, RQ$=75\cdot1$ (SD$=5\cdot2$). The difference is probably greater because of the 24 pupils, there were 10 in Sec 3 who had the minimum RQ of 70 minus, compared with 6 in P7. The conclusion remains the same, those pupils who were receiving remedial teaching in P7 made some progress between P7 and Sec 3, but relatively less than their contemporaries. This applied whether the pupils were in remedial classes in secondary school or not.

Remedial classes in secondary schools

The secondary schools operated three systems of organization for the less academically able pupils. One was streaming, or allocating the pupils to classes taking courses at a level appropriate to their ability. Another was the addition of small 'remedial' classes to a set of classes of mixed and generally equal ability. The third was withdrawal from the normal classes of selected pupils for special teaching. In the last, the arrangements were so flexible, pupils being withdrawn for different reasons at different times in the school session and for different lengths of time, that comparison of the progress of these pupils with those in established remedial classes was not possible.

In the secondary schools there have always been those pupils whose academic performance has been clearly below average. At different times these pupils have been designated 'non-passers', 'article 14c', and 'modified'. The current designation for the classes containing such pupils is 'remedial'. Apart from the results of an unproductive primary education, it is not clear what is being remedied. Remedial classes could be identified in seven secondary schools with 136 pupils in nine classes of average size of 15 pupils. It is these classes whose progress is examined here, having in mind that though reading is not the only basis of allocation to remedial classes, it is the largest single component.

Of the 136 pupils in Remedial classes, 90 had been tested in P7, 56 boys and 34 girls. In P7, the mean reading quotient of these pupils was $RQ=77 \cdot 8$ ($SD=11 \cdot 8$) and the mean VRQ was $VRQ=80 \cdot 1$ ($SD=8 \cdot 1$). The difference between mean RQ and VRQ is not significant. The attainment and ability of these pupils is clearly below average.

The 64 pupils who were tested again in Sec 3 had a mean $RQ=78 \cdot 0$ ($SD=7 \cdot 9$). The average reading quotients in P7 and Sec 3 are virtually identical, so these pupils in the small Remedial classes have not progressed relative to their contemporaries in other classes. The majority took Stage 3 Reading Test.

The policy of remedial classes in first and second year secondary school seems to have departed a long way from the concept of remedial teaching designed to give help to pupils whose attainments appear to be out of step with their estimated ability. The remedial classes appear to be constituted on the principle of establishing remedial classes with a given number of places, and filling these places with the pupils whose attainments fall most noticeably below the level of their contemporaries. The withdrawal system is closest to the conditions in the primary school, but because of its flexibility it is not possible, short of accumulating large numbers of individual case histories, to reach general findings about its practices and effectiveness.

In secondary school the smaller remedial classes appear to maintain the relative reading standards of their pupils, but there is no evidence of improvement.

Conclusions and observations

The provisions for remedial teaching of reading appear as confused both in policy and practice. Although during the three years of the investigation there were changes in school staffing and provisions, there was, nevertheless, no evidence that special remedial provisions were either equitably distributed over the schools, or clearly related to the needs of the pupils. In fact, a large proportion, 44 per cent in P5 for example, of the pupils considered to need remedial teaching were given this by their class teachers only, and appeared by P7 to have suffered no disadvantage therefrom when compared with those receiving special remedial teaching in addition to normal class teaching.

There was also a lack of clarity in regard to the criteria by which pupils were selected for remedial teaching. The pupils could be selected on the basis of discrepancy between their reading attainment and the best estimate of their abilities. This would not only involve more careful diagnosis than is at present supplied, but would also imply that pupils of various levels of reading attainment would be referred to receive teaching appropriate to their needs. Alternatively, the pupils could be selected on the basis of discrepancy between their reading progress and that of the remainder of the class, the purpose being to relieve the class teacher of the extra time and effort required to attend to pupils whose progress is either extremely fast or extremely slow. The question to be resolved is whether the main function of the remedial teacher is to assist the pupils or assist the teachers. In the ultimate analysis the ends are the same, but the means are very different. In practice, adequate diagnosis of individual reading difficulties is seriously inadequate, and pupils with specific difficulties related to reading, and pupils of average or above average reading attainments are swamped by the large number of pupils referred for remedial teaching, because their standard is unacceptably low for their class. The average reading quotient of remedial pupils is $RQ=79$ ($SD=9$) and fewer than one per cent of them have RQ of 100 or over. Boys predominate to the extent of at least 55 per cent to 45 per cent girls, and the mean RQ of boys is $RQ=80$, and of girls $RQ=77$. Is there a behaviour component here?

The picture that emerges is that of remedial teaching confined to pupils of clearly below average attainment, and no systematic diagnosis made to distinguish between pupils with specific disabilities and those who occupy the lower places in the normal distribution of ability and attainment. The evidence on the effectiveness of special remedial teaching of reading is, as could be inferred from the selection criteria, not encouraging. Of the pupils receiving remedial teaching in P4, eleven were considered to need no further remedial teaching in P5 and P6, finishing with an acceptable average level of attainment in P7 of $RQ=89$. A parallel group of twenty-five pupils continued to receive remedial teaching in P5 and P6, finishing in P7 with average $RQ=78$, virtually what they began with. It is not being stated here that all pupils receiving remedial teaching show no improvement in their level of attainment. The question rather is whether there is an unacceptably high proportion who do not, even after three or two years of continuous remedial teaching, and whether remedial teachers are wasting time, effort and money in maintaining such pupils in remedial groups for such a long period. In round figures, about a quarter of the remedial pupils seem to become permanent inhabitants of remedial groups for two or three years, with no evidence of improvement in status. It is doubtful if this is the most profitable use of remedial teachers.

In secondary schools the withdrawal of selected pupils for remedial teaching as and when considered necessary is allied to the system in primary schools, and to a large extent shares its advantages and defects. Again, there is little evidence of adequate diagnosis and selected pupils are almost entirely of a below average reading attainment. The alternative system of creating small 'remedial' classes is even more haphazard. The basic procedure appears to be that the number and size of these classes is determined, then on the information available the pupils of lowest scholastic attainment are allocated to these classes till the full complement has been reached. The prevailing practice is to aim at 15 pupils, who proceed through a basic course at less than the normal rate, receiving individual tuition to a greater extent than in other classes. The name 'remedial' for these classes seems an inappropriate one.

Accepting the dictionary definition of remedial as having some relevance to educational practice, it would seem that the most effective use of remedial reading services would involve:

(a) the identification of pupils whose reading attainments are markedly discrepant from their other school work, or from the average standard of their class or age group. These pupils would not be the poor readers only;

(b) a much more thorough diagnosis of the degree and nature of the pupils' disabilities, to enable the remedial teachers immediately to direct their activities along the lines where they are likely to be most effective;

(c) more intensive remedial teaching of pupils referred for special tuition. The current average of about 30 minutes per week seems scarcely adequate. Regular reviews of the pupils' progress seems necessary, and pupils not progressing or not showing signs of progressing should be returned to the normal activities of the classroom. The practice of retaining pupils for remedial teaching for periods of up to three years would need very strong justification;

(d) the continuation of the primary school pattern of remedial teaching into the secondary school. Diagnosis of individual difficulties in secondary pupils seems even more superficial than in primary school, and with the wider range of reading skills required, the case for skilled guidance in reading and study skills is even stronger. Though it lies outwith the scope of this inquiry, there is evidence that concentration of remedial help in the upper secondary classes on those pupils preparing for higher education would seem profitable.

Though remedial teaching of reading falls within the scope of this inquiry, it was not the intention to devote a disproportionate amount of attention to the five per cent or so of the pupils receiving or needing special remedial teaching. The conclusions reached are not the outcome of an exhaustive investigation into that particular component of the teaching of reading. What does emerge is not comforting, and calls both for a review of the policy of remedial teaching, especially of reading, and a more thorough investigation of the practice and its effectiveness. It is common for research reports to recommend further research, but in this instance it seems to be needed.

Chapter 12

Review and Recommendations

'I will end heir . . . wishing yow, docile Reidar, als gude success and greit proffeit by reiding this short treatise as I tuke earnist and willing panis to blok it, as ye sie, for your cause. Fare weill.' *James VI of Scotland and I of England: Ane Schort Treatise conteining some reulis and cautelis to be observit and eschewit in Scottis Poesie.*

In this investigation three streams of pupil reading activity have been identified, the mainly literary style which is taught as 'Reading', the functional reading required for school studies other than English, and the leisure reading of the pupils. The plan of the investigation was to follow a representative selection of classes and pupils over two three year periods, from Primary 4 to Primary 7, and from Primary 7 to Secondary 3. By putting the two samples end on, a survey of progress from P4 to Sec 2 inclusive is possible, and by administering a standardized reading test at the beginning and end of each three-year span, progress and final attainment can be assessed. The reading progress and attainment can be assessed both for pupils, where fuller investigation has been conducted into those defined as good or poor readers, and for classes, which are the natural units at least for primary school pupils.

The progress of pupils in the three main streams can also be considered in terms of intake, that is the characteristics of the pupils as received by the teachers, and of treatment, that is the educational practices, attitudes and policies of the teachers over the span of the inquiry. It became clear during the inquiry that the nature of the intake, in terms of differences in pupils' ability and home background, far outweighed differences in teaching practices in determining progress and attainment in reading. The differences in reading attainment of pupils within classes were significantly greater than differences between classes, and even with the narrower range of differences between classes, the classes which were above average in P4 tended to remain above average in P7, and similarly for below average classes. The allocation of secondary pupils to classes of mixed and equal ability precludes similar analysis for secondary schools, but again differences between the average reading attainments of secondary schools are small compared to the range of pupils' attainments within schools. In short, there were no schools or classes, apart from the grant-aided schools where pupils were selected, and apparently effectively selected, on scholastic ability, which could be identified as good or poor with the same substantial differences as distinguish the pupils selected as good or poor readers. Differences in reading attainment are influenced mainly by factors out-with the control of the teachers.

The teaching of 'reading'

The teaching of that style of reading, mainly narrative/descriptive/comprehension, which is the core of primary school reading and of the English teaching in secondary schools, appears as being done effectively and adequately. The reading tests used were mainly, but not wholly, concerned with this kind of reading, and there is no evidence of any decline in reading standards at the end of primary education during the period of this inquiry. In the early secondary classes, even the poorer readers in P7 show some improvement in reading standard by the time they have reached third year secondary. There is no accepted definition of illiteracy, but on a best estimate based on reading test scores, the amount of illiteracy at the end of the primary school, and of the first two years of secondary schooling is very small, of the order of one per cent of pupils, and few of the one per cent are wholly illiterate.

Though teachers may be disappointed to find that the investigation has revealed no method or combination of practices which result in better reading attainment than others, the most likely explanation of this is that there are no such methods and in fact current practices are equally effective.

Recommendation (1) is that it would be more profitable for teachers and others involved in education to direct their attention to those more neglected aspects of reading than to pursue more detailed inquiries into minor differences of methods and materials used in the teaching of the kind of reading under discussion here.

There is one current trend, however, that needs watching closely. There is consistent evidence, for example from Kent (Dr J. Morris) and from Inner London (Dr A. Little) that class size, up to current limits of about 45 pupils per teacher, is not related to the attainments or progress of the pupils in school subjects. This investigation confirms the findings, that class size is irrelevant to reading attainment and progress in the primary school. There is at present pressure to reduce class sizes, and the first effects are beginning to appear in Table 2.6. The reduction of class size in the primary schools by the creation of composite classes is accompanied by a reduction in the reading standards of these classes.

Recommendation (*2*) is that the effects of reducing class sizes by creating smaller classes of pupils at different stages should be kept under close review, with particular reference to the standards in reading.

Recommendation (*3*) is that an alternative practice of fewer classes per teacher should be set up for a pilot inquiry, to ascertain whether more teacher time for preparation, correction and the like may lead to better progress and attainment by the pupils.

Functional reading

If the teaching of the basically literary style of reading can be described as satisfactory, the same cannot be said for the teaching of the skills involved in functional reading, which plays a central part in school studies. There has been in the primary schools, and to a lesser extent in the secondary schools a movement towards less direct class teaching and to a greater amount of individual and group learning, where pupils are given a greater amount of freedom and responsibility in their learning. This tendency does not appear to be accompanied by a corresponding development in the teaching of the study and reading techniques necessary to make those changes in teaching methods effective. In the older arithmetic teaching, the reading of 'problems' was a difficulty, but in the more recent style of mathematics in the primary school, the reading element is more widespread throughout the subject. About a quarter of the primary teachers complained of reading difficulties with mathematics texts, but a more objective assessment of readability level lent no support to this view. The reading level appeared as no different from that of the class readers. The reasons for this difficulty are not immediately obvious from the evidence presented in this investigation, but it appeared from the interviews with teachers that many teachers assumed that the reading learned from class readers would transfer to the different kind of reading required for other text books. Some did arrange preparation for reading of mathematics; others met the difficulty by preparing their own work cards. Another reason for the difficulty appeared to be that teachers did not consider reading as an integral part of other studies, or to put it crudely, took the view that reading was reading and maths was maths.

The other area involving functional reading was in the work by the pupils on projects, assignments or topics. There was little evidence of direct teaching of the reading styles of selective reading, rapid skimming or adequate reference skills. As there skills are the basis for later school study, and for any studies pursued after school, their importance and value increases as the pupils move through the educational system. There seems no reason why the better readers at least should not begin acquiring these reading and study skills in P4 or P5 classes. The amount of functional reading required of upper primary school pupils in class and for homework is probably as much as in class 'reading' periods, and should be given equal attention. The principal inadequacy was that many teachers did not appreciate that good reading was the style of reading best adapted to the purpose of reading and the type of material to be read, and that the pupil who has learned to read fluently and intelligently from a class reader is not necessarily equipped to tackle the kinds of reading required for effective study in other contexts. The need appears to be for more guidance, exercise and especially approval for different reading styles. Those teachers who were more aware of the needs complained, with justification, of the lack of reading material comparable in variety and supply to class readers.

Recommendation (4) is that there is need for research into and development of methods and reading material aimed at developing the functional reading skills.

Recommendation (5) is that steps be taken in the training, both pre-service or in-service, of primary school teachers to emphasize the need for a wider and more flexible approach to the teaching of reading as an integral part of all school learning.

In the secondary school the problem is the same, though the context is different. Here, the reading requirements vary from one subject area to another, and no single teacher is responsible for the teaching of the appropriate reading skills. Whether this would best be done by the subject teachers giving greater attention to reading and study skills, or by English teachers extending their activities beyond basically literary studies, or by remedial or guidance teachers extending their scope, remains an open question. It has to be kept in mind that in many kinds or work, styles of reading other than literary are occupational skills, and deserve attention as such. Also there are complaints from universities and colleges about deficiencies in reading and study abilities of pupils proceeding to higher education.

Recommendation (6) is that there should be in each secondary school a member or members of staff with necessary additional training whose duty it would be to develop the reading and study skills of the pupils, appropriate to the subject requirements and level of study.

Leisure reading

In one week at the end of May, 2004 primary 7 pupils recorded 4082 books as having been read by them, and 2370 pupils of the same classes recorded 10,186 comics, newspapers and magazines as having been read during the same week. This represents a very considerable amount of reading, and though an exact estimate is difficult, it is quite probable that most pupils do more reading outside the classroom than within it. Also, judging from the kind of material read, it is probable that this kind of reading will continue after the reading requirements of the school have come to an end. Leisure reading, whether of books or comics, cannot be ignored as a major part of the process of learning to read.

'Does the road wind uphill all the way? Yes, to the very end.' These words of Christina Rosetti apply to the reading taught in school, where progression is the rule. But they do not seem to apply to leisure reading, in which there appears very little progression between the upper primary and lower secondary classes for most pupils. The language level of the leisure reading material is not low; it is the content that seems to be the main source of objection. Nevertheless, if pupils by their own choice read a substantial amount outside of school requirements, there seems little reason for discouraging them, and if they obtain substantial measure of enjoyment from their reading there is still less reason. If pupils cannot use the reading skill they have acquired to enjoy their reading, a large element in the reasons for teaching them to read disappears.

How far disapproval (and it exists) influences pupils' leisure reading is uncertain. But the exercise of their reading abilities on congenial material cannot be wholly bad for pupils. Lateral reading, the extension of reading activities to material within the compass of the pupils' abilities, can be as helpful in establishing a habit of reading as progressive reading, where the pupils are continuously being called upon to develop further skills. The increasing separation between leisure reading and school interests may be one fruit of teacher disapproval. Teacher encouragement is another matter. Too much may link leisure reading with school reading, with its necessary elements of prescription and progression. But it could be that the drop in reading related to school activities, which appears in the secondary school, is related to the situation that there is no longer a single teacher to show interest in pupils' private reading. The boundary between encouragement of leisure reading whether rubbishy or not, and pupil interpretation of it as interference is a very narrow one. But if appreciation of 'good' literature is being developed within school, it does not seem necessary to pursue it into the home and playground as well.

Recommendation (7) is that the teaching of reading in both primary and secondary schools should be accompanied by judicious interest by teachers in pupils' leisure reading, regardless of its literary quality.

Good and poor readers

When members of the investigating Unit visited schools the commonest response in secondary schools was to refer to the remedial and English teachers. Requests to discuss teaching of reading with for example maths or domestic science teachers was readily agreed to, but not suggested by the schools. In primary schools the Unit were referred to class teachers and remedial teachers if such were available. In the majority of secondary schools, classes other than remedial were of mixed and equal ability, so that there was an identifiable group of poor readers, but no corresponding group of good readers. In the primary there was a corresponding group of poor readers, needing but not always receiving special remedial teaching, in whom the class teachers showed considerable interest and about whose personal characteristics and home conditions the class teachers often had extensive information to offer. The same was not apparent for good readers, who were often accepted as a welcome bonus by the teachers, but who were not the subjects of the same interest and attention. To have relied on the class teachers submissions to produce comparable groups of poor and good readers would have resulted in a smallish group of identified poor readers, of almost uniformly low reading attainment, but without any comparable identifiable group of good readers. To secure comparable groups for the purpose of isolating and contrasting as fully as possible, balanced groups of good and poor readers were selected on the basis of the initial reading test scores of the pupils, and their characteristics, particularly their socioeconomic background, examined more fully.

The characteristics and progress of the pupils selected by schools as requiring special remedial teaching, mainly of reading, are described in a previous chapter. The evidence reveals this aspect of the teaching of reading as being the least satisfactory. That a number of pupils receiving special remedial teaching do return to normal class teaching with an acceptable level of reading attainment is not to be denied, but there does seem to be an unacceptably large number of primary pupils who remain in remedial groups for several school sessions and who show little apparent benefit from it. In the secondary school remedial classes, pupils appear to be assigned to them for two or more years, and if any disabilities are being remedied, there seems little provision for such pupils to be returned to 'normal' classes.

The findings of this inquiry are best summed up in a series of recommendations.

Recommendation (8) is that provisions be made for much more thorough diagnosis both on entry to and return from any special remedial teaching.

Recommendation (9) is that an investigation be made to ascertain with what range of ability within a class the class teacher can effectively cope.

Recommendation (10) is that the remedial teaching of pupils referred for such should be more intensive than at present, and pupils' progress should be reviewed at regular and frequent intervals.

Recommendation (11) is that in secondary schools, and to some extent in upper primary classes, remedial reading services should be used to develop the reading skills of those pupils aiming to enter higher education or occupations in which reading is a necessary skill.

Recommendation (12) is that current remedial reading provisions and practices should be reviewed with the aim of providing appropriate assistance to pupils of all levels of reading attainment and ability, and not as at present only those of low reading attainment.

The good and poor readers selected for study were classified on two bases, those good or poor with reference to the two sample populations, and those good or poor with reference to their P4 or P7 classes. The second group was selected for study because, being in the same school classes, the educational environment was constant, and factors other than school practices could be more easily identified. As it turned out, the main factors associated with good or poor reading attainment were outwith the school's control, being mainly intellectual ability, home background and to a lesser measurable extent, motivation. These were related to the two groups of good and poor readers in much the same way, so distinctions between the groups are only marginal.

In interpreting the results of the good and poor reader part of the inquiry, it must be kept in mind that though there is an association between social class and reading attainment, there is a large amount of exception to the general relationship. Also, differences in proportions and differences in absolute numbers are not the same. Though a higher proportion of pupils in Social Classes I and II may be good readers than in Class III Manual, yet on average the teachers are likely to find more good readers in their classes from Class III Manual homes than from Class I and II homes, because there are more of the former in the school population. The other point that emerges is that good and poor readers are not mirror images of each other; each have their own characteristics and must be considered separately.

Most of the distinctions between good and poor readers in relation to social background generally appear to have been established by the time pupils reach P4, and progress thereafter is more closely related to the nature of the intake than to variations in educational treatment. Social background can be considered in terms of the school neighbourhood and of the home. There is a relationship between attainment of the intake P4 pupils and the socioeconomic character of the neighbourhood, independent of the social class of the home, but this is not maintained when pupils' progress from P4 to P7 is considered. Only the pupils of non-manual workers' homes show progress related to poor or good school neighbourhood. Alteration of school catchment areas to provide a greater 'social mix' would leave children of manual workers unaffected, and probably penalize the children of non-manual workers in the better neighbourhoods. Conversely, transfer of children from a poor to a better school neighbourhood would benefit pupils from non-manual homes, but not the others.

In the secondary school, differences in home background are most marked amongst the good readers. Home encouragement appears as a significant factor, as does transfer of reading from comics to magazines and newspapers. Book reading distinguishes primary school good and poor readers independently of social class, but in secondary classes book reading is not a major difference between good and poor readers.

Intelligence, home encouragement, social class, school neighbourhood and leisure reading all appear as powerful predictors of reading attainment, and by primary 4 the broad patterns of distinction between good and poor readers appear to have been established. What has been analysed in this report are differences in rate of progress rather than success or failure in learning to read. Such changes as can be identified are taking place in a context of general progress of reading competence, and variations in school practices and policies appear to have little influence on differences in reading progress. The pupils appearing as most sensitive to environmental conditions are the good readers and those from non-manual households. It is here that teachers may be able to assist pupils by appropriate support and encouragement.

Envoi

Perhaps by now the 'docile Reidar' will have formed his or her conclusions about the lessons to be learned from these investigations, which may not wholly agree with those presented in the report. There can be differences in the interpretation of evidence and emphasis. The interpretation here is based on the view that the essence of effective teaching is that the pupils should know what they have to do, should know how to do it, should know when it is done and should know how well it has been done. Also, the report subscribes to the policy that children should be educated according to their age, aptitude and ability, and that this includes good readers.

INDEX